Bible Promises
for Parents of Children
with Special Needs

Bible Promises

for parents of children with
SPECIAL NEEDS

AMY E. MASON

Tyndale House Publishers, Inc.
Carol Stream, Illinois

Visit Tyndale online at www.tyndale.com.

TYNDALE and Tyndale's quill logo are registered trademarks of Tyndale House Publishers, Inc.

Bible Promises for Parents of Children with Special Needs

Designed by Nicole Grimes

For information about special discounts for bulk purchases, please contact Tyndale House Publishers at csresponse@tyndale.com or call 800-323-9400.

ISBN 978-1-4964-1727-5

Printed in the United States of America

23	22	21	20	19	18	17
7	6	5	4	3	2	1

Contents

Introduction

⚓

Caring for someone with special needs is an incredible journey. At times the road can be lonely and difficult to navigate, while at other times it brings joy and victory. The unique situations you face as a parent of a child with special needs may leave you wondering, *Is the Bible relevant for me?* The answer is an overwhelming *yes*!

Hidden within the pages of Scripture are beautiful stories of people with special needs. Jesus met children and adults with all kinds of disabilities, and we find comfort in the way he noticed their condition and responded with compassion. His attention to each situation shows the intrinsic value of every person with special needs. These stories offer hope because God notices and pursues you and your child too, and he walks with you on this awesome adventure.

Bible Promises for Parents of Children with Special Needs is a topical guide to God's promises. Each topic was selected for its relevance to parents or caregivers of a person with special needs. You will find Scripture promises that speak to the uniqueness of special needs parenting—both the joys and the struggles. These promises offer you comfort and x | BIBLE PROMISES . . .

encouragement. They are truths to celebrate, and they lay a foundation for hope. Claim them as your own. Pray them over your family and over your children. Let them guide you into the presence of Jesus.

Does your heart ever ache with questions, confusion, or discouragement? Caring for a child with autism, Down syndrome, cerebral palsy, ADHD, emotional or behavioral disorders, physical disabilities, or learning disabilities can be all-consuming. Do you ever feel you have no margin in your schedule and no emotional reserves? Do you long for encouragement, rest, and refreshment? Scripture speaks hope into your weariness and struggles.

While there are times of difficulty on your journey, there are also times of great joy! When your heart is full of love and bursts with pride for your child, when your child reaches a new milestone, achieves a new skill, or exceeds all expectations—go to Scripture, which speaks of celebration, joy, and gratitude as well.

Focusing on God's promises ushers you into his presence. Claiming God's promises for your everyday life helps you become aware of his passion for you and for your child. Jesus came to offer an abundant, satisfying life filled with joy (John 10:10). As you explore these promises, my prayer is that you'll discover God's provision for you in every moment.

ABANDONMENT

When you feel like God has abandoned you . . .

- PSALM 9:10 | Those who know your name trust in you, for you, O LORD, do not abandon those who search for you.

- 2 CORINTHIANS 4:9 | We are hunted down, but never abandoned by God. We get knocked down, but we are not destroyed.

- JOHN 14:16 | I will ask the Father, and he will give you another Advocate, who will never leave you.

As a parent of a child with special needs, do you ever feel alone? In your difficult times, some of your closest friends may neglect or even desert you, but God never will. He is always pursuing you, trying to get your attention. Are you aware of him? If you are sincerely looking for God, you are sure to find him because he will never abandon anyone who wants a relationship with him. In fact, your difficulties can help you look more intently for God so that you can see him—right by your side.

ABILITIES

When you feel unqualified to meet your family's needs . . .

- 2 CORINTHIANS 3:5-6 | It is not that we think we are qualified to do anything on our own. Our qualification comes from God. He has enabled us to be ministers of his new covenant. This is a covenant not of written laws, but of the Spirit. The old written covenant ends in death; but under the new covenant, the Spirit gives life.

When you come to the end of your own abilities . . .

- ISAIAH 40:29-31 | He gives power to the weak and strength to the powerless. Even youths will become weak and tired, and young men will fall in exhaustion. But those who trust in the LORD will find new strength. They will soar high on wings like eagles. They will run and not grow weary. They will walk and not faint.

- ZECHARIAH 4:6 | It is not by force nor by strength, but by my Spirit, says the LORD of Heaven's Armies.

When people focus on what your child may never do . . .

- MATTHEW 19:26 | Jesus looked at them intently and said, "Humanly speaking, it is impossible. But with God everything is possible."

- EPHESIANS 3:20 | Now all glory to God, who is able, through his mighty power at work within us, to accomplish infinitely more than we might ask or think.

Parents of children with special needs often talk about abilities. You are probably keenly aware of both your child's ability level and your own. However, the end of your abilities may be when you're able to see God's power and strength most clearly. When others focus on what your child cannot do, see it as an opportunity to focus on who God is and what *he* can do through you and your child. Sometimes inability is the vehicle for experiencing the blessing of God's powerful presence and provision.

ABUNDANCE
When you need more than others can give . . .

- EPHESIANS 3:18-19 | May you have the power to understand, as all God's people should, how wide, how long, how high, and how deep his love is. May you experience the love of Christ, though it is too great to understand fully. Then you will be made complete with all the fullness of life and power that comes from God.

When it feels as if everything is being taken away . . .

- ROMANS 5:20 | God's law was given so that all people could see how sinful they were. But as people sinned more and more, God's wonderful grace became more abundant.

- PSALM 36:7-9 | All humanity finds shelter in the shadow of your wings. You feed them from the abundance of your own house, letting them drink from your river of delights. For you are the fountain of life, the light by which we see.

- JOHN 10:10 | The thief's purpose is to steal and kill and destroy. My purpose is to give them a rich and satisfying life.

When you need confidence that God loves you abundantly . . .

- 1 JOHN 4:9-10 | God showed how much he loved us by sending his one and only Son into the world so that we might have eternal life through him. This is real love—not that we loved God, but that he loved us and sent his Son as a sacrifice to take away our sins.

The more stressful life is, the harder it is for us to be generous. Not so with God. When the human heart starts tightening under pressure, God's heart releases love and grace. There is more than enough in God's economy. His love is wide and deep and full, and it overflows upon you. It overflows upon your child, as well. So open your heart to him and let his love fill you up. He is ready to offer you a purposeful, abundant life!

ACCEPTANCE
When you're having trouble accepting your situation . . .

- 1 CORINTHIANS 7:17; ROMANS 8:18, 23 | Each of you should continue to live in whatever situation the Lord has placed you, and remain as you were when God first called you . . . [for] what we suffer now is nothing compared to the glory he will reveal to us later. . . . And we believers also groan, even though we have the Holy Spirit within us as a foretaste of future glory, for we long for our bodies to be released from . . . suffering. We, too, wait with eager hope for the day when God will give us our full rights as his adopted children, including the new bodies he has promised us.

When your family has trouble accepting your child's diagnosis . . .

- ROMANS 15:7 | Accept each other just as Christ has accepted you so that God will be given glory.

When your child isn't accepted by his peers . . .

- GALATIANS 2:20 | I live in this earthly body by trusting in the Son of God, who loved me and gave himself for me.

- PSALM 25:14 | The LORD is a friend to those who fear him.

- PSALM 23:6 | Surely your goodness and unfailing love will pursue me all the days of my life.

Special needs may present you and your child with some challenging circumstances. Coming to grips with this reality is a constant process of embracing your situation while maintaining hope in God and his promises. It's okay to struggle to accept your circumstances, and it's okay when other people struggle with this too. We live in a fallen world where everybody faces unbelievably hard situations. In fact, the Bible says difficulty is to be *expected*. Times of challenge are when you need hope, and hope comes both from looking forward to heaven and also realizing that God brings good from your adversity here on earth. Each day you live in the continuing trials of life. When you keep eternity in mind, you can grow from the trials you experience, knowing that your difficult circumstances will end with this earthly life.

———————————❖———————————

ADOPTION

When adopting a child with special needs becomes part of your family's story . . .

- EPHESIANS 1:4-5 | Even before he made the world, God loved us and chose us in Christ to be holy and without fault in his eyes. God decided in advance to adopt us into his own family by bringing us to himself through Jesus Christ. This is what he wanted to do, and it gave him great pleasure.

- PSALM 113:7-9 | He lifts the poor from the dust and the needy from the garbage dump. He sets them among princes, even the princes of his own people! He gives the childless woman a family, making her a happy mother.

When people question your decision to adopt . . .

- PSALM 127:3 | Children are a gift from the LORD; they are a reward from him.

- MATTHEW 18:5 | [Jesus said,] "Anyone who welcomes a little child like this on my behalf is welcoming me."

When I forget that God has adopted me . . .

- GALATIANS 3:26 | You are all children of God through faith in Christ Jesus.

- JOHN 1:12 | To all who believed him and accepted him, he gave the right to become children of God.

- GALATIANS 4:4-5 | When the right time came, God sent his Son, born of a woman, subject to the law. God sent him to buy freedom for us who were slaves to the law, so that he could adopt us as his very own children.

Adoption is a wonderful expression of God's love. You, too, are God's adopted child. He thought of you before you came to him. He loved you, chose you, sacrificed for you, and has given you all of the rights and privileges of being his child. God's children have all kinds of strengths and needs. You and your child are part of God's amazing love story.

ADVICE

When you don't know how to evaluate all the advice you're getting from others . . .

- PSALM 119:105 | Your word is a lamp to guide my feet and a light for my path.

- JAMES 1:5 | If you need wisdom, ask our generous God, and he will give it to you. He will not rebuke you for asking.

- PSALM 37:30 | The godly offer good counsel; they teach right from wrong.

- JOHN 16:13 | When the Spirit of truth comes, he will guide you into all truth.

When you feel confused and pulled by a multitude of suggestions about how to care for your child, don't forget the necessity of taking all of this to God in prayer. To hear God's voice clearly, it is important to read the Bible because this is how he speaks to you. If you trust Jesus as your Savior, you have the Holy Spirit, who is called the Counselor. Also, seek out godly people who have a gift for giving wise counsel, who have proven themselves to be faithful, honest, and trustworthy. They can be counted on to give you wisdom that lines up with God's Word.

ADVOCATE

When your family needs an advocate . . .

- JOHN 14:16-17 | I will ask the Father, and he will give you another Advocate, who will never leave you. He is the Holy Spirit, who leads into all truth. The world cannot receive him, because it isn't looking for him and doesn't recognize him. But you know him, because he lives with you now and later will be in you.

When you need someone to fight for your family . . .

- EXODUS 14:14 | The LORD himself will fight for you. Just stay calm.

- 2 CHRONICLES 20:15 | Don't be discouraged . . . for the battle is not yours, but God's.

You're never left to fight life's battles alone. When you're parenting a child with special needs, you may sometimes feel you have to fight tooth and nail to get the help and care your child needs and deserves. Whether you're just worn out or there's no one who can help or seems to understand, God is always your Advocate. He's with you now, ready to guide and encourage you. Let the Lord fight your battles for you. He is on your side and will give you victory!

AFFIRMATION

When you're longing for some affirmation . . .

- EPHESIANS 2:10 | We are God's masterpiece. He has created us anew in Christ Jesus, so we can do the good things he planned for us long ago.

- 1 THESSALONIANS 1:4 | We know, dear brothers and sisters, that God loves you and has chosen you to be his own people.

- 1 PETER 5:10 | In his kindness God called you to share in his eternal glory by means of Christ Jesus. So after you have suffered a little while, he will restore, support, and strengthen you, and he will place you on a firm foundation.

When you know your child needs more affirmation . . .

- EPHESIANS 4:29 | Let everything you say be good and helpful, so that your words will be an encouragement to those who hear them.

- COLOSSIANS 1:11 | We also pray that you will be strengthened with all his glorious power so you will have all the endurance and patience you need.

- PROVERBS 15:30 | A cheerful look brings joy to the heart.

We all have a need to feel affirmed, to know that our life has value and is valued by others. Sadly, people don't always offer the affirmation we need, and as a result we might feel rejected, alone, or worthless. When no one else offers words of affirmation, you and your child can feel affirmed that an almighty God chose to create you both in his image and wants you to be in relationship with him. God draws you to himself, even to the point of sacrificing his own Son to die for your sins so that you can have the opportunity to live with him forever. God's words and actions toward you affirm that he desires a relationship with you more than anything else and that you matter to him.

AMBIGUITY

When there's no clear path in front of you . . .

- PSALM 147:5 | How great is our Lord! His power is absolute! His understanding is beyond comprehension!

- PROVERBS 20:24 | The LORD directs our steps, so why try to understand everything along the way?

- PSALM 32:8 | The LORD says, "I will guide you along the best pathway for your life. I will advise you and watch over you."

- PSALM 37:23 | The LORD directs the steps of the godly. He delights in every detail of their lives.

- ROMANS 8:28 | We know that God causes everything to work together for the good of those who love God and are called according to his purpose for them.

You can be sure God's character is not ambiguous—he always acts justly and consistently. But God's ways may be unpredictable and mysterious. When you're not sure about the next step for your child with special needs, trust that God knows and that his plans often surprise us and even defy human logic. The unexplainable aspects of God teach us to respect him and show him the reverence he deserves. When you wonder what the future holds for you and your family, you need not doubt that God is always at work in your life, redeeming whatever heartache and adversity the enemy has brought against you.

ANGER

When you wonder if God is angry with you . . .

- PSALM 103:8-10 | The LORD is compassionate and merciful, slow to get angry and filled with unfailing love. He will not constantly accuse us, nor remain angry forever. He does not punish us for all our sins; he does not deal harshly with us, as we deserve.

- PSALM 30:5 | His anger lasts only a moment, but his favor lasts a lifetime! Weeping may last through the night, but joy comes with the morning.

When people take their anger out on you . . .

- PROVERBS 15:1 | A gentle answer deflects anger, but harsh words make tempers flare.

When anger gets the best of you . . .

- JAMES 1:19-21 | Understand this, my dear brothers and sisters: You must all be quick to listen, slow to speak, and slow to get angry. Human anger does not produce the righteousness God desires. So . . . humbly accept the word God has planted in your hearts, for it has the power to save your souls.

When you feel angry with God about your circumstances . . .

- 2 CORINTHIANS 12:7-10 | I was given a thorn in my flesh. . . . I begged the Lord to take it away. Each time he said, "My grace is all you need. My power works best in weakness." So now I am glad . . . about my weaknesses, so that the power of Christ can work through me. . . . For when I am weak, then I am strong.

When you are holding a grudge against someone else . . .

- MARK 11:25-26 | When you are praying, first forgive anyone you are holding a grudge against, so that your Father in heaven will forgive your sins, too.

- GENESIS 50:20; ROMANS 8:28 | You intended to harm me, but God intended it all for good. . . . God causes everything to work together for the good of those who love God.

Angry feelings can erupt when you're under too much stress—and as a special needs parent, you may experience an enormous amount of stress. Sometimes your anger is targeted at another; sometimes it's aimed at God. Sometimes it's really not targeted at anyone at all, just your circumstances. God understands because even he experiences anger over injustice, suffering, and the struggles of so many in this fallen world. Fortunately, God's anger is always righteous. He loves you so much that he gets angry when you have to suffer, especially when you are a victim of circumstances beyond your control. When you get angry, this is the kind of anger you must have—not anger that stems from self-pity or that lashes out and hurts others. As a parent of a child with special needs, you have no doubt experienced anger in your own heart or taken the brunt of another's anger. Let God be your model for the right kind of anger—and for how you can use it to comfort those in need and work to fight injustice. Let him be your steady source of love to check a bruised ego, a flaring temper, or a broken heart. He is your means to forgiveness and the way to a tranquil soul.

APATHY

When you're at a point where you just don't care anymore . . .

- HEBREWS 2:1 | We must listen very carefully to the truth we have heard, or we may drift away from it.

- HEBREWS 6:10-12 | God is not unjust. He will not forget how hard you have worked for him and how you have shown your love to him by caring for other believers, as you still do. Our great desire is that you will keep on loving others as long as life lasts, in order to make certain that what you hope for will come true. Then you will not become spiritually dull and indifferent.

When you want to stop feeling apathetic . . .

- PHILIPPIANS 2:4, 13 | Don't look out only for your own interests, but take an interest in others, too. . . . For God is working in you, giving you the desire and the power to do what pleases him.

When apathy settles in your heart, you often feel listless as passion and purpose drain away. Apathy is like a disease that feeds on your cares and motivations and wastes your talents and gifts. Fortunately, there is an antidote. God promises that as you turn your heart toward him and return to his Word, you will remember the purposes for which he made you. Then your passion for life and family will be renewed and the characteristics of a purposeful life—meaningful work, a thankful heart, and acts of service—will be restored.

ASSUMPTIONS

When others make wrong assumptions about your child . . .

- 1 CORINTHIANS 4:5 | Don't make judgments about anyone ahead of time—before the Lord returns. For he will bring our darkest secrets to light and will reveal our private motives. Then God will give to each one whatever praise is due.

- 1 PETER 5:10 | In his kindness God called you to share in his eternal glory by means of Christ Jesus. So after you have suffered a little while, he will restore, support, and strengthen you, and he will place you on a firm foundation.

- 2 PETER 1:2 | May God give you more and more grace and peace as you grow in your knowledge of God and Jesus our Lord.

You have probably run into people who make assumptions about you or your child. Maybe you have been judged for being a bad parent without someone knowing your child has special needs. Or perhaps people assume your child can't relate to others just because he or she can't speak well or interacts differently. Either way, they don't know your story. This is a good lesson for you, too, because it can help you realize that you may not know their story either. What fears drive their actions? What hurts do they carry? When people falsely assume things about you, it doesn't have to shake you because *you* know you and your child are part of God's glorious story. When you remember what it feels like to deal with wrong assumptions, you can respond graciously and continue to parent with confidence that God knows you and cares for you.

ATTITUDE

When you see others suffer and it's hard to feel positive . . .

- 2 CORINTHIANS 1:3-5 | God is our merciful Father and the source of all comfort. He comforts us in all our troubles so that we can comfort others. . . . For the more we suffer for Christ, the more God will shower us with his comfort through Christ.

When you want to change your thoughts . . .

- PHILIPPIANS 4:8-9 | Now, dear brothers and sisters, one final thing. Fix your thoughts on what is true, and honorable, and right, and pure, and lovely, and admirable. Think about things that are excellent and worthy of praise. Keep putting into practice all you learned and received from me—everything you heard from me and saw me doing. Then the God of peace will be with you.

- ROMANS 12:2 | Don't copy the behavior and customs of this world, but let God transform you into a new person by changing the way you think. Then you will learn to know God's will for you, which is good and pleasing and perfect.

When there is tension in your home and you want to set a peaceful tone . . .

- ROMANS 15:5-6 | May God, who gives this patience and encouragement, help you live in complete harmony with each other, as is fitting for followers of Christ Jesus. Then all of you can join together with one voice, giving praise and glory to God, the Father of our Lord Jesus Christ.

When you wonder what attitude pleases God . . .

- ROMANS 8:5-6 | Those who are dominated by the sinful nature think about sinful things, but those who are controlled by the Holy Spirit think about things that please the Spirit. . . . Letting the Spirit control your mind leads to life and peace.

- ROMANS 14:17-18 | The Kingdom of God is not a matter of what we eat or drink, but of living a life of goodness and peace and joy in the Holy Spirit. If you serve Christ with this attitude, you will please God.

- HEBREWS 13:16 | Don't forget to do good and to share with those in need. These are the sacrifices that please God.

When life is smooth sailing, it's easier to stay positive. But when days are hard and troubles loom, it's difficult to focus on anything except the problem and your own feelings about it. Your circumstances have a powerful ability to influence your attitude. God understands this and offers advice for setting a joyful tone in your home each day: Meditate on what is good and positive, and think about encouraging others through words and acts of service. When you practice these things consistently, it becomes easier to have a positive attitude that is more powerful than your circumstances. When you live to serve Christ with this kind of attitude, you will experience more of his joy and peace.

BEAUTY
When you've lost your sense of wonder . . .

- ISAIAH 35:2 | Yes, there will be an abundance of flowers and singing and joy! The deserts will become as green as the mountains of Lebanon, as lovely as Mount Carmel or the plain of Sharon. There the LORD will display his glory, the splendor of our God.

- NEHEMIAH 8:10 | Go and celebrate with a feast . . . and share gifts of food with people who have nothing prepared. This is a sacred day . . . the joy of the LORD is your strength!

- ECCLESIASTES 3:11 | God has made everything beautiful for its own time. He has planted eternity in the human heart, but even so, people cannot see the whole scope of God's work from beginning to end.

Learning to find beauty in life is one of the best ways to prepare your heart and mind for moments with God. Good times on earth are a taste of heaven. But in the midst of daily routines and weariness, beauty and wonder are hard to see—they can seem hidden to your senses. Restoring your sensitivity to God's beauty won't happen in an instant. Think about one thing that most inspires your senses. Look for that one thing each day until you rediscover the wonder of it. This will help you when you're dealing with the difficult circumstances of life.

BEGINNINGS

When nothing new seems to be happening . . .

- HEBREWS 3:14 | If we are faithful to the end, trusting God just as firmly as when we first believed, we will share in all that belongs to Christ.

- ZECHARIAH 4:10 | Do not despise these small beginnings, for the LORD rejoices to see the work begin.

When you dare to hope that this could be the start of something new . . .

- PHILIPPIANS 1:6 | I am certain that God, who began the good work within you, will continue his work until it is finally finished on the day when Christ Jesus returns.

- LAMENTATIONS 3:23 | Great is his faithfulness; his mercies begin afresh each morning.

When you wonder what the future holds for your child . . .

- REVELATION 21:5 | The one sitting on the throne said, "Look, I am making everything new!"

It's not a matter of whether change will come but how you will deal with it when it does. You are probably more accustomed to new beginnings than you think, for each day brings new challenges and problems. Each day also brings new opportunities to get to know God better and to start over with a new attitude toward your current circumstances. Because God's mercies begin fresh every single day, you don't have to be burdened by yesterday's failures or regrets. So embrace the dawn of each new day as a divine moment, a chance to start again and to experience the refreshing mercies of God—both for yourself and your family.

BEHAVIOR

When your child's behavior is crushing your spirit . . .

- PSALM 34:18 | The LORD is close to the brokenhearted; he rescues those whose spirits are crushed.

- PSALM 73:26 | My health may fail, and my spirit may grow weak, but God remains the strength of my heart; he is mine forever.

- PSALM 119:116 | LORD, sustain me as you promised, that I may live! Do not let my hope be crushed.

When you're shocked by your own behavior . . .

- EPHESIANS 1:4-6 | Even before he made the world, God loved us and chose us in Christ to be holy and without fault in his eyes. God decided in advance to adopt us into his own family by bringing us to himself through Jesus Christ. This is what he wanted to do, and it gave him great pleasure. So we praise God for the glorious grace he has poured out on us who belong to his dear Son.

- ROMANS 8:1 | There is no condemnation for those who belong to Christ Jesus.

When you're tired of evaluating your child solely by her behavior . . .

- 1 JOHN 3:1 | See how very much our Father loves us, for he calls us his children, and that is what we are!

- 1 SAMUEL 16:7 | People judge by outward appearance, but the LORD looks at the heart.

Behavior is one way to measure progress, and as a special needs parent, you may spend a lot of time observing and assessing your child's behaviors. If you struggle with your child's difficult behavior, make sure your hope is more firmly attached to the Lord than it is to your child's progress. When you feel crushed by your child's behavior, ask God to help you see her through his eyes and to focus on her heart more than her actions. Ask him to give you fresh eyes for your child so that you will be able to respond with love.

BITTERNESS

When you resent your friends for having children without special needs . . .

- PROVERBS 14:30 | A peaceful heart leads to a healthy body; jealousy is like cancer in the bones.

- HEBREWS 12:15 | Look after each other so that none of you fails to receive the grace of God. Watch out that no poisonous root of bitterness grows up to trouble you, corrupting many.

When you resent your spouse for dealing with things differently . . .

- COLOSSIANS 3:13-15 | Make allowance for each other's faults, and forgive anyone who offends you. Remember, the Lord forgave you, so you must forgive others. Above all, clothe yourselves with love, which binds us all together in perfect harmony. And let the peace that comes from Christ rule in your hearts. For as members of one body you are called to live in peace. And always be thankful.

- EPHESIANS 4:31-32 | Get rid of all bitterness, rage, anger, harsh words, and slander, as well as all types of evil behavior. Instead, be kind to each other, tender-hearted, forgiving one another, just as God through Christ has forgiven you.

When you can't stop dwelling on your hurt . . .

- PROVERBS 27:3-4 | A stone is heavy and sand is weighty, but the resentment caused by a fool is even heavier. Anger is cruel, and wrath is like a flood, but jealousy is even more dangerous.

- MARK 11:25 | When you are praying, first forgive anyone you are holding a grudge against, so that your Father in heaven will forgive your sins, too.

- ISAIAH 26:3 | You will keep in perfect peace all who trust in you, all whose thoughts are fixed on you!

- TITUS 1:15 | Everything is pure to those whose hearts are pure.

Nothing robs you of more joy than unresolved anger. When anger is dwelled on and not dealt with, it leads to bitterness and resentment. The antidotes to bitterness are contentment and forgiveness. First, instead of focusing on the parenting situation others have, try to think of how you are blessed in your own parenting journey. As you become more aware of the good things God has done for you, you are less likely to feel angry and offended. Second, nothing is more liberating than forgiveness. Forgiveness not only frees the offender but it unburdens you as well. It opens up your heart to connection again—especially connection with God. Yes, sometimes being a parent of a child with special needs can be a catalyst for pain. When you are hurt, let your thoughts focus on God and his blessings in your life so that you can move from anger to forgiveness and live out the incredible, unburdened story God has planned for you and your family.

BLAME

When you blame yourself for what has happened . . .

- 1 CORINTHIANS 1:8 | He will keep you strong to the end so that you will be free from all blame on the day when our Lord Jesus Christ returns.

- COLOSSIANS 1:22 | He has reconciled you to himself through the death of Christ in his physical body. As a result, he has brought you into his own presence, and you are holy and blameless as you stand before him without a single fault.

- EPHESIANS 1:4 | Even before he made the world, God loved us and chose us in Christ to be holy and without fault in his eyes.

- ISAIAH 50:7 | Because the Sovereign LORD helps me, I will not be disgraced. Therefore, I have set my face like a stone, determined to do his will. And I know that I will not be put to shame.

When your pain makes you want to point the finger at someone else . . .

- MATTHEW 5:44-45 | [Jesus said,] "Love your enemies! Pray for those who persecute you! In that way, you will be acting as true children of your Father in heaven.

For he gives his sunlight to both the evil and the good, and he sends rain on the just and the unjust alike."

- JAMES 4:12 | God alone, who gave the law, is the Judge. He alone has the power to save or to destroy. So what right do you have to judge your neighbor?

When facing disappointment, you might condemn yourself, ask the *what if* questions, or focus on *if only* thoughts that lead to regret. It's so easy to blame yourself when your child faces challenges you didn't expect, or when nothing you try seems to help. When assigning blame dominates your thoughts, your perspective becomes negative, which leads to discouragement, depression, anger, shame, and bitterness. Stop the blame game. God doesn't want you to dwell on what could have been; he wants you to focus on what can be. He is the God of hope who gives you the gift of his approval.

❖

BLESSINGS

When you need to see how God is going to bring good through your circumstances . . .

- EPHESIANS 1:3 | All praise to God, the Father of our Lord Jesus Christ, who has blessed us with every spiritual blessing in the heavenly realms because we are united with Christ.

- JAMES 1:12 | God blesses those who patiently endure testing and temptation. Afterward they will receive the crown of life that God promised to those who love him.

- 1 CORINTHIANS 15:57-58 | Thank God! He gives us victory over sin and death through our Lord Jesus Christ. So, my dear brothers and sisters, be strong and immovable. Always work enthusiastically for the Lord, for you know that nothing you do for the Lord is ever useless.

- GALATIANS 6:9 | Let's not get tired of doing what is good. At just the right time we will reap a harvest of blessing if we don't give up.

Blessings aren't only the material kind; the greatest blessings are far more valuable than money or possessions. They come in the form of joy, family, relationships, a peaceful heart, comfort, and the confidence of eternal life. When you belong to Christ, you understand that all you are and all you have is a gift from him, to be used to bless others. Focus on what God has already done for you, and then use your current circumstances to encourage and help others (especially other parents who have children with special needs). As you bless them, you will begin to see the amazing good that can come from your difficult situation.

BROKENNESS

When your heart breaks for your child . . .

- PSALM 22:24 | He has not ignored or belittled the suffering of the needy. He has not turned his back on them, but has listened to their cries for help.

When your heart is broken over sin . . .

- ISAIAH 44:22 | I have swept away your sins like a cloud. I have scattered your offenses like the morning mist. Oh, return to me, for I have paid the price to set you free.

When you feel overwhelmed by pain or grief . . .

- PSALM 34:18 | The LORD is close to the brokenhearted; he rescues those whose spirits are crushed.

- PSALM 147:3 | He heals the brokenhearted and bandages their wounds.

- Psalm 31:7 | I will be glad and rejoice in your unfailing love, for you have seen my troubles, and you care about the anguish of my soul.

When you feel like you are falling apart, there are three things you can be absolutely sure of. First, God is with you. Even though it may feel like he is far away, the fact is that he's right by your side. Second, God both sees and hears you. Not a tear can fall without God noticing. Third, God cares deeply. He cares so much that he not only walks with you through the burdens and the pain, but he also made a way to freedom for you through the death and resurrection of Jesus. You can be confident because Jesus has already provided the way to eternal life, where there will be no more pain, suffering, or broken hearts.

BUSYNESS
When you can't seem to get it all done . . .

- Proverbs 31:17, 27 | She is energetic and strong, a hard worker. . . . She carefully watches everything in her household and suffers nothing from laziness.

- Matthew 11:28-29 | Jesus said, "Come to me, all of you who are weary and carry heavy burdens, and I will give you rest. Take my yoke upon you. Let me teach you, because I am humble and gentle at heart, and you will find rest for your souls."

When your child won't let you sit still . . .

- PSALM 23:2-3 | He lets me rest in green meadows; he leads me beside peaceful streams. He renews my strength.

Let's face it—life as the parent of a child with special needs is going to be busy because you have so many extra things to do. You have to accept that there may be extra activity for you and that your schedule may almost always be full. The key is to stay close to God so he can give you a clear sense of your calling and the wisdom to discern which things are worth doing and which you should let go. And then you need to be disciplined about finding some time—even if it is small snatches of a few minutes—when you can sit with God and his Word and let him speak to you with his assurance of love, comfort, and peace of mind and heart. The peace he offers will give you a sense of confidence about what you can let go, and it will allow you to actually enjoy the everyday tasks.

CARING

When you wonder if God cares about your circumstances . . .

- PSALM 31:7 | I will be glad and rejoice in your unfailing love, for you have seen my troubles, and you care about the anguish of my soul.

- PSALM 145:18-19 | The LORD is close to all who call on him. . . . He hears their cries for help and rescues them.

- 1 PETER 5:7 | Give all your worries and cares to God, for he cares about you.

- PSALM 91:11 | He will order his angels to protect you wherever you go.

When you wonder if *you* care anymore . . .

- 1 CORINTHIANS 15:58 | My dear brothers and sisters, be strong and immovable. Always work enthusiastically for the Lord, for you know that nothing you do for the Lord is ever useless.

- PSALM 68:19 | Praise the Lord; praise God our savior! For each day he carries us in his arms.

When you wonder how to teach your child to be caring . . .

- PSALM 57:2 | I cry out to God Most High, to God who will fulfill his purpose for me.

God's love for you began before you were born, continues throughout your life, and extends through eternity. Since he created you to have a relationship with him, he cares about every detail of your life. He knows all your troubles and hurts, and he takes care of you during them. God's care for you is your model and inspiration for caring for others with compassion, especially your child with special needs.

CELEBRATION

When you're ready to celebrate . . .

- DEUTERONOMY 12:7 | There you and your families will feast in the presence of the LORD your God, and you will rejoice in all you have accomplished because the LORD your God has blessed you.

When you need a reason to celebrate . . .

- 1 CORINTHIANS 15:57 | Thank God! He gives us victory over sin and death through our Lord Jesus Christ.

- REVELATION 21:4 | He will wipe every tear from their eyes, and there will be no more death or sorrow or crying or pain. All these things are gone forever.

When celebrations are different or difficult for your family . . .

- ISAIAH 49:13 | Sing for joy, O heavens! Rejoice, O earth! Burst into song, O mountains! For the LORD has comforted his people and will have compassion on them in their suffering.

- REVELATION 19:6-7 | Praise the LORD! For the Lord our God, the Almighty, reigns. Let us be glad and rejoice, and let us give honor to him.

Are holidays and celebrations difficult for you and your family because of your child's special needs? It's helpful to be reminded of why God wants you to celebrate. What makes a celebration unique is that you take time out from the ordinary to honor a special person or a notable event. God gives you the ultimate reason to celebrate because he has rescued you from the consequences of sin and shown you the wonders of eternity. Celebration is a powerful way to increase your hope because it takes your focus off your troubles and puts it on God's blessings—and ultimately on God himself. Those who love him truly have the most to celebrate!

CHANGE

When you wonder if you can deal with any more change . . .

- HEBREWS 13:8 | Jesus Christ is the same yesterday, today, and forever.

- LAMENTATIONS 5:19 | LORD, you remain the same forever! Your throne continues from generation to generation.

- JAMES 1:17 | Whatever is good and perfect is a gift coming down to us from God our Father. . . . He never changes or casts a shifting shadow.

When your child needs help coping with changes . . .

- PSALM 3:3 | You, O LORD, are a shield around me; you are my glory, the one who holds my head high.

- DEUTERONOMY 31:8 | Do not be afraid or discouraged, for the LORD will personally go ahead of you. He will be with you; he will neither fail you nor abandon you.

Change is one of the great constants of life. It happens to everyone, whether because of the slow, gradual erosion of time or the swift, cataclysmic moments of trauma. People change, children grow, schools diversify, technology advances—indeed, life itself can be described as a process of continual change. Some changes are positive: a new friend, a good teacher, a financial windfall, a new therapy for your child that seems to help. Other changes are negative: a tragic loss, a job layoff, a setback with your child. Either way, change can be stressful. But God is changeless and dependable. You can count on his love, his comfort, and his promises no matter what happens to you and your family.

CHILDREN

When you wonder what God has in store for your child . . .

- MARK 10:14 | [Jesus] said to them, "Let the children come to me. Don't stop them! For the Kingdom of God belongs to those who are like these children."

- PSALM 121:8 | The LORD keeps watch over you as you come and go, both now and forever.

- PROVERBS 20:24 | The LORD directs our steps, so why try to understand everything along the way?

- JEREMIAH 29:11 | "For I know the plans I have for you," says the LORD. "They are plans for good and not for disaster, to give you a future and a hope."

When you feel like you're the only one looking out for your child . . .

- ISAIAH 40:11 | He will feed his flock like a shepherd. He will carry the lambs in his arms, holding them close to his heart. He will gently lead the mother sheep with their young.

When you fear for your child . . .

- PROVERBS 14:26 | Those who fear the LORD are secure; he will be a refuge for their children.

When you are overwhelmed with love for your child . . .

- PSALM 127:3 | Children are a gift from the LORD; they are a reward from him.

Children hold a special place in God's heart, just as they do in the hearts of their parents. Children of all abilities are gifts from the Lord. As a parent, you open that gift continually as you seek the Lord and point your children to Jesus. He holds your children close to his heart, he is their place of safety, and his arms are always open to them.

CHURCH

When you wonder what your church can do to help . . .

- JAMES 1:5 | If you need wisdom, ask our generous God, and he will give it to you. He will not rebuke you for asking.

- 1 JOHN 3:16-17 | We know what real love is because Jesus gave up his life for us. So we also ought to give up our lives for our brothers and sisters. If someone has enough money to live well and sees a brother or sister in need but shows no compassion—how can God's love be in that person?

- ROMANS 12:13; 15:5-6 | When God's people are in need, be ready to help them. . . . May God, who gives this patience and encouragement, help you live in complete harmony with each other, as is fitting for followers of Christ Jesus. Then all of you can join together with one voice, giving praise and glory to God, the Father of our Lord Jesus Christ.

When you wonder if your child is welcome at church . . .

- 1 CORINTHIANS 12:14, 26-27 | Yes, the body has many different parts, not just one part. . . . If one part suffers, all the parts suffer with it, and if one part is honored, all the parts are glad. All of you together are Christ's body, and each of you is a part of it.

- 1 CORINTHIANS 12:18-22 | Our bodies have many parts, and God has put each part just where he wants it. How strange a body would be if it had only one part! Yes, there are many parts, but only one body. The eye can never say to the hand, "I don't need you." The head can't say to the feet, "I don't need you." In fact, some parts of the body that seem weakest and least important are actually the most necessary.

Your child is an important part of the family of God. When the church neglects someone with disabilities, it is like neglecting a necessary part of its own body, and all the parts suffer because of it. The church needs you and your child. If you feel the church could do more to support you and other families with special needs, start by asking God for wisdom about what could be done or how to humbly approach someone in leadership. Many families have tangible needs that the church can meet, such as meals or companionship. Perhaps God wants to use your family to help other children with special needs feel welcome in the church and to find new ways of ministering to other families in your situation.

COMFORT

When you're grieving . . .

- MATTHEW 5:4 | God blesses those who mourn, for they will be comforted.

- PSALM 34:18 | The LORD is close to the brokenhearted; he rescues those whose spirits are crushed.

When you need someone to be present with you . . .

- PSALM 23:4 | Even when I walk through the darkest valley, I will not be afraid, for you are close beside me. Your rod and your staff protect and comfort me.

When you need to hear words of peace . . .

- PSALM 119:52 | I meditate on your age-old regulations; O LORD, they comfort me.

- PHILIPPIANS 4:6-7 | Don't worry about anything; instead, pray about everything. . . . Then you will experience God's peace, which exceeds anything we can understand. His peace will guard your hearts and minds as you live in Christ Jesus.

- PSALM 29:11 | The LORD gives his people strength; the LORD blesses them with peace.

When your child needs to be comforted and you have nothing left to give . . .

- PSALM 18:32 | God arms me with strength, and he makes my way perfect.

- PSALM 94:19 | When doubts filled my mind, your comfort gave me renewed hope and cheer.

- 2 CORINTHIANS 1:3-4 | All praise to God, the Father of our Lord Jesus Christ. God is our merciful Father and the source of all comfort. He comforts us in all our troubles so that we can comfort others. When they are troubled, we will be able to give them the same comfort God has given us.

Although the troubles in your heart can make you feel far from God, his promises reassure you that he is nearest in times of trouble and brokenness. God shows up every time you need comfort—not with presents but with his *presence.* It is God's presence, and knowing he is beside you, that settles your soul in the moments of your very worst distress.

COMPARISONS

When you feel like you don't measure up to other parents . . .

- PSALM 119:5 | Oh, that my actions would consistently reflect your decrees!

- 2 CORINTHIANS 3:18 | All of us who have had that veil removed can see and reflect the glory of the Lord. And the Lord—who is the Spirit—makes us more and more like him as we are changed into his glorious image.

- 1 JOHN 3:2 | Dear friends, we are already God's children, but he has not yet shown us what we will be like when Christ appears. But we do know that we will be like him, for we will see him as he really is.

- GALATIANS 6:4-5 | Pay careful attention to your own work, for then you will get the satisfaction of a job well done, and you won't need to compare yourself to anyone else. For we are each responsible for our own conduct.

When you're frustrated that your child isn't like other kids . . .

- PSALM 139:13-14 | You made all the delicate, inner parts of my body and knit me together in my mother's womb. Thank you for making me so wonderfully complex! Your workmanship is marvelous—how well I know it.

- PSALM 128:1, 3-4 | How joyful are those who fear the LORD—all who follow his ways! . . . Your children will be like vigorous young olive trees as they sit around your table. That is the LORD's blessing for those who fear him.

How do I measure up? is a question most of us grapple with. Satan tries to convince us to compare ourselves to other people, telling us that our worth is based on how we measure up in appearance, possessions, accomplishments, or social status. Whether we're comparing ourselves or our child, this usually leaves us feeling either inadequate and envious or puffed up with pride. In God's eyes, every person is valued and loved, so there's no reason for comparisons. A better way is to maintain balance between humility over sin and exultation in God's lavish grace. God doesn't compare you with others, so neither should you. Just enjoy his grace, which has no comparison.

COMPASSION

When you wonder if God is moved by your struggles . . .

- PSALM 72:13-14 | He feels pity for the weak and the needy, and he will rescue them. He will redeem them from oppression . . . for their lives are precious to him.

- PSALM 145:9 | The LORD is good to everyone. He showers compassion on all his creation.

- PSALM 103:13 | The LORD is like a father to his children, tender and compassionate to those who fear him.

When you see your child's great need . . .

- 1 JOHN 3:16 | We know what real love is because Jesus gave up his life for us. So we also ought to give up our lives for our brothers and sisters.

You may have experienced the pain of people who have zero compassion for you or your child. But as a special needs family, you are also uniquely equipped to understand the challenges of other families who have children with special needs. Jesus was moved to action by humanity's struggles. Ask God to fill your heart with his compassion for others.

CONDEMNATION

When others misjudge you because of your child's behavior and you're feeling condemned . . .

- JAMES 4:12 | God alone, who gave the law, is the Judge. He alone has the power to save or to destroy. So what right do you have to judge your neighbor?

- ROMANS 14:10 | Why do you condemn another believer? Why do you look down on another believer? Remember, we will all stand before the judgment seat of God.

- ROMANS 8:1 | Now there is no condemnation for those who belong to Christ Jesus.

- ROMANS 8:31, 33-34 | What shall we say about such wonderful things as these? If God is for us, who can ever be against us? . . . Who dares accuse us whom God has chosen for his own? No one—for God himself has given us right standing with himself. Who then will condemn us? No one—for Christ Jesus died for us and was raised to life for us, and he is sitting in the place of honor at God's right hand, pleading for us.

- EPHESIANS 2:10 | We are God's masterpiece. He has created us anew in Christ Jesus, so we can do the good things he planned for us long ago.

There is a difference between condemnation, discipline, and accountability. Condemnation is judgmental—it focuses on an assumption of wrongdoing. Discipline is restorative, focusing on loving correction. Accountability is focused on encouraging others to do what is right. Someone who does not have a child with special needs will most likely not understand that traditional methods of discipline or accountability may not work with your child, and they may be tempted to judge you according to the norm. This is where you need to keep your attention focused on God, who has given you the confidence to know with certainty that he sees you and your child as his masterpieces and that he does not condemn you.

CONTENTMENT

When the world tells you that you need more . . .

- PSALM 90:14 | Satisfy us each morning with your unfailing love, so we may sing for joy to the end of our lives.

- HEBREWS 13:5 | Don't love money; be satisfied with what you have. For God has said, "I will never fail you. I will never abandon you."

When you want more or better for your family . . .

- PHILIPPIANS 4:11-13 | I have learned how to be content with whatever I have. I know how to live on almost nothing or with everything. I have learned the secret of living in every situation, whether it is with a full stomach or empty, with plenty or little. For I can do everything through Christ, who gives me strength.

When you wonder if God can satisfy the desires of your heart . . .

- PSALM 107:8-9 | Let them praise the LORD for his great love and for the wonderful things he has done for them. For he satisfies the thirsty and fills the hungry with good things.

Contentment can't be gained by owning more, being more, or doing more. Contentment comes through your relationship with Jesus Christ. What you lack, he has stored up in abundance. What you long for, he can satisfy. When you feel discontent with your situation or with your family, view it as an invitation to bring your feelings before God and exchange them for the fullness of his love and contentment for today.

CONTROL

When your world is falling apart . . .

- COLOSSIANS 1:17 | He existed before anything else, and he holds all creation together.

- JOHN 10:27-30 | [Jesus said,] "My sheep listen to my voice; I know them, and they follow me. I give them eternal life, and they will never perish. No one can snatch them away from me, for my Father has given them to me, and he is more powerful than anyone else. No one can snatch them from the Father's hand. The Father and I are one."

When you feel like your family is controlled by special needs . . .

- EPHESIANS 1:21 | He is far above any ruler or authority or power or leader or anything else—not only in this world but also in the world to come.

- PSALM 138:8 | The LORD will work out his plans for my life.

When you can't restrain your emotions . . .

- ROMANS 8:6 | Letting your sinful nature control your mind leads to death. But letting the Spirit control your mind leads to life and peace.

- GALATIANS 5:22-23 | The Holy Spirit produces this kind of fruit in our lives: love, joy, peace, patience, kindness, goodness, faithfulness, gentleness, and self-control.

When your child behaves in ways you cannot control . . .

- PHILIPPIANS 3:21 | He will take our weak mortal bodies and change them into glorious bodies like his own, using the same power with which he will bring everything under his control.

Have you ever been late for an appointment because you were stuck in traffic? Have you watched your child struggle to master a concept that other children her age understand easily? Has your child ever melted down at exactly the time you needed him not to? Sooner or later we all face situations beyond our control. The Bible teaches that even when we find ourselves in unpredictable, uncontrollable, and frustrating circumstances, there is one thing we can control: our reaction to the situation. We can trust God to work in our lives to bring order, hope, and peace out of chaos. It may feel like you're in a free fall right now, but God has not let go. All things are under his control, and his goal is closeness with you. When your life starts spinning or your child's needs seem like more than you can handle, God is holding it all together. In his eyes, the shambles of your life look like the pieces to a beautiful puzzle.

CRISIS
When you feel like you're moving from one crisis to another . . .

- JOHN 16:33 | I have told you all this so that you may have peace in me. Here on earth you will have many trials and sorrows. But take heart, because I have overcome the world.

- PSALM 46:1-3, 7 | God is our refuge and strength, always ready to help in times of trouble. So we will not fear when earthquakes come and the mountains crumble into the sea. Let the oceans roar and foam. Let the mountains tremble as the waters surge! . . . The LORD of Heaven's Armies is here among us.

Even though Jesus warns us that troubles in this life are inevitable, most of us still get caught off guard when a crisis comes. We live in a fallen world, and if we're raising a child with special needs, the difficulties might seem a little more frequent. Jesus' words in John 16:33 offer comfort, showing that your struggles aren't out of the ordinary. What is extraordinary is that God is with you in your crises. He also promises that these struggles will not have the final word because he has overcome them. God's promise of victory helps protect your heart from discouragement when you're facing a crisis.

DEATH

When you search for hope in the face of death . . .

- 1 CORINTHIANS 15:43 | Our bodies are buried in brokenness, but they will be raised in glory. They are buried in weakness, but they will be raised in strength.

- ROMANS 8:38 | I am convinced that nothing can ever separate us from God's love. Neither death nor life.

When you fear death . . .

- 1 CORINTHIANS 15:54-57 | When our dying bodies have been transformed into bodies that will never die, this Scripture will be fulfilled: "Death is swallowed up in victory. O death, where is your victory? O death, where is your sting?" For sin is the sting that results in death, and the law gives sin its power. But thank God! He gives us victory over sin and death through our Lord Jesus Christ.

- PSALM 23:4 | Even when I walk through the darkest valley, I will not be afraid, for you are close beside me.

When you've lost someone you love . . .

- MATTHEW 5:4 | God blesses those who mourn, for they will be comforted.

When you worry about who will care for your child when you're gone . . .

- MATTHEW 6:26, 28-30 | [Jesus said,] "Look at the birds. They don't plant or harvest or store food in barns, for your heavenly Father feeds them. And aren't you far more valuable to him than they are? . . . And why worry about your clothing? Look at the lilies of the field and how they grow. They don't work or make their clothing, yet Solomon in all his glory was not dressed as beautifully as they are. And if God cares so wonderfully for wildflowers that are here today and thrown into the fire tomorrow, he will certainly care for you."

- JOHN 14:16 | [Jesus said,] "I will ask the Father, and he will give you another Advocate, who will never leave you."

- PSALM 78:72 | He cared for them with a true heart and led them with skillful hands.

- PSALM 121:7-8 | The LORD keeps you from all harm and watches over your life. The LORD keeps watch over you as you come and go, both now and forever.

- ISAIAH 51:8 | My righteousness will last forever. My salvation will continue from generation to generation.

The Bible has a great deal to say about death—and what is on the other side of it. It is clear that God cares deeply about both those who die and their loved ones who outlive them. His care extends from generation to generation, and your child is included in that promise! Those who believe Scripture's message will find great hope instead of fear and despair. Jesus, by dying for our sins and rising from the dead, has shown us how to triumph over death. All who trust in him will share in that victory!

DECISIONS
When it feels as if you have no options . . .

- LAMENTATIONS 3:22-23 | The faithful love of the LORD never ends! His mercies never cease. Great is his faithfulness; his mercies begin afresh each morning.

- PSALM 18:30, 36 | God's way is perfect. All the LORD's promises prove true. He is a shield for all who look to him for protection. . . . You have made a wide path for my feet to keep them from slipping.

When you need God's direction moment by moment . . .

- PSALM 37:23 | The LORD directs the steps of the godly. He delights in every detail of their lives.

- JAMES 1:5 | If you need wisdom, ask our generous God, and he will give it to you.

When you're making a major decision . . .

- PROVERBS 3:5-6 | Trust in the LORD with all your heart; do not depend on your own understanding. Seek his will in all you do, and he will show you which path to take.

We make hundreds, if not thousands, of decisions each day, some as small as choosing between chocolate or vanilla ice cream and some as big as whom to marry, what job to take, where to live, or what kind of treatment to pursue for your child. The most important decision you will ever make is how you respond to Jesus. If you choose to believe that he is who he says he is, it will affect and dramatically impact all other decisions, including those you make regarding your children.

DELIVERANCE

When you long for God to set your child free from his or her struggles . . .

- REVELATION 21:3-4 | I heard a loud shout from the throne, saying, "Look, God's home is now among his people! He will live with them, and they will be his people. God himself will be with them. He will wipe every tear from their eyes, and there will be no more death or sorrow or crying or pain. All these things are gone forever."

- 2 CORINTHIANS 12:7-10 | I was given a thorn in my flesh. . . . I begged the Lord to take it away. Each time he said, "My grace is all you need. My power works best in weakness." So now I am glad . . . about my weaknesses, so that the power of Christ can work through me. . . . For when I am weak, then I am strong.

- MALACHI 4:2 | For you who fear my name, the Sun of Righteousness will rise with healing in his wings. And you will go free, leaping with joy like calves let out to pasture.

When you are waiting for God's deliverance . . .

- ISAIAH 51:1, 5 | Listen to me; all who hope for deliverance—all who seek the LORD! . . . My mercy and justice are coming soon. My salvation is on the way. My strong arm will bring justice to the nations. All distant lands will look to me and wait in hope for my powerful arm.

The struggles of special needs in a family can make you long for a miracle. Let this longing lead you closer to God.

God can deliver your child from bondage in this life; but if he does not, be assured that for all eternity your child will be safe and free from any suffering and limitations.

DIAGNOSIS

When you receive a new diagnosis . . .

- ROMANS 8:16 | His Spirit joins with our spirit to affirm that we are God's children.

- ROMANS 8:35, 37 | Can anything ever separate us from Christ's love? Does it mean he no longer loves us if we have trouble or calamity, or are persecuted, or hungry, or destitute, or in danger, or threatened with death? . . . No, despite all these things, overwhelming victory is ours through Christ, who loved us.

When you wonder if your child's special needs are somehow your fault . . .

- JOHN 9:3 | "It was not because of his sins or his parents' sins," Jesus answered. "This happened so the power of God could be seen in him."

When you're worried a diagnosis will define your child . . .

- COLOSSIANS 3:11 | In this new life, it doesn't matter if you are a Jew or a Gentile, circumcised or uncircumcised, barbaric, uncivilized, slave, or free. Christ is all that matters, and he lives in all of us.

Every person and every family has struggles. A diagnosis can certainly change your life, but it doesn't change your or your child's identity as a child of God—loved and rescued by Jesus Christ. Help your child see his worth through God's eyes.

DISABILITIES

When you wonder how God views children with disabilities . . .

- HEBREWS 4:15-16 | This High Priest of ours understands our weaknesses, for he faced all of the same testings we do, yet he did not sin. So let us come boldly to the throne of our gracious God. There we will receive his mercy, and we will find grace to help us when we need it most.

- 1 CORINTHIANS 12:7 | A spiritual gift is given to each of us so we can help each other.

- Isaiah 35:5-6 | When he comes, he will open the eyes of the blind and unplug the ears of the deaf. The lame will leap like a deer, and those who cannot speak will sing for joy!

- Luke 7:22 | Then he told John's disciples, "Go back to John and tell him what you have seen and heard—the blind see, the lame walk, those with leprosy are cured, the deaf hear, the dead are raised to life, and the Good News is being preached to the poor."

So many people go through life with the special challenge of physical, mental, or emotional disabilities. Yet these disabilities by no means negate the fact that they are loved and valued by God, who has a unique purpose for each person. The Bible gives us many examples of how to relate to those who have disabilities. It's a great mistake when people see these individuals as less than human, fail to engage them in their lives, or believe they can't learn from them. God sees the value in all his people and offers everyone the opportunity to experience his healing, mercy, and salvation. As a parent or caregiver of a child with special needs, you understand this, but many still don't. Your child could be the door through which others gain this understanding.

DISCOURAGEMENT

When you start to doubt that progress is possible . . .

- ISAIAH 35:3-6 | With this news, strengthen those who have tired hands, and encourage those who have weak knees. Say to those with fearful hearts, "Be strong, and do not fear, for your God is coming to destroy your enemies. He is coming to save you." And when he comes, he will open the eyes of the blind and unplug the ears of the deaf. The lame will leap like a deer, and those who cannot speak will sing for joy!

When your child regresses . . .

- PSALM 73:26 | My health may fail, and my spirit may grow weak, but God remains the strength of my heart; he is mine forever.

- 2 CORINTHIANS 4:8-9, 18 | We are pressed on every side by troubles, but we are not crushed. We are perplexed, but not driven to despair. . . . We get knocked down, but we are not destroyed. . . . So we don't look at the troubles we can see now; rather, we fix our gaze on things that cannot be seen. For the things we see now will soon be gone, but the things we cannot see will last forever.

- ROMANS 5:3-4 | We can rejoice, too, when we run into problems and trials, for we know that they help us develop endurance. And endurance develops strength of character, and character strengthens our confident hope of salvation.

When you lose confidence . . .

- 2 THESSALONIANS 2:16-17 | Now may our Lord Jesus Christ himself and God our Father, who loved us and by his grace gave us eternal comfort and a wonderful hope, comfort you and strengthen you in every good thing you do and say.

- ISAIAH 43:2 | When you go through deep waters, I will be with you. When you go through rivers of difficulty, you will not drown. When you walk through the fire of oppression, you will not be burned up; the flames will not consume you.

Discouragement can seem like a constant companion as you fight for your child's health or work for her to gain skills. When you are discouraged, you can be in danger of giving up—on God, friends, family, even hope itself. It can feel like everyone's against you and nobody cares. Worst of all, you may not be able to see the way back to joy and happiness. What you do at this low point will determine whether you sink deeper in the mire or begin to climb your way back up. God is your greatest encourager. Seek his advice first. Seek the counsel of others who can help you put things in perspective, face what has brought you low, and plan the steps to recover. When you see a way out, that is the divine moment when hope returns—and over time, your joy will return too. Each setback is a chance for God to aid and comfort you. Backward steps are part of the journey, but God never makes you walk alone.

DOUBT

When you begin to doubt if God is in this journey with you . . .

- LUKE 1:37 | The word of God will never fail.

- LUKE 12:31-32 | Seek the Kingdom of God above all else, and he will give you everything you need. So don't be afraid, little flock. For it gives your Father great happiness to give you the Kingdom.

- HEBREWS 13:5 | God has said, "I will never fail you. I will never abandon you."

- GENESIS 18:14 | Is anything too hard for the LORD?

- PSALM 94:19 | When doubts filled my mind, your comfort gave me renewed hope and cheer.

Doubt can be a trapdoor to fear, or it can be a doorway to confident faith. When you doubt God's ability to help you in the face of great odds but you trust him anyway and he acts, your faith is strengthened. God wants you to express your faith in him *before* he acts. So when God calls you to keep going, don't be surprised if at first it seems like the obstacles are stacking up. This may be a test of your faith. God may be preparing to deepen your faith and strengthen your character so that you know it is really God—rather than your own efforts—who is coming to your rescue. When the task ahead of you seems too big and you doubt your ability to see it through, that is the time to trust him to work through you.

DREAMS

When you surrender your dreams to the Lord . . .

- EPHESIANS 3:20 | Now all glory to God, who is able, through his mighty power at work within us, to accomplish infinitely more than we might ask or think.

When you need a new dream . . .

- PSALM 37:4-5 | Take delight in the LORD, and he will give you your heart's desires. Commit everything you do to the Lord. Trust him, and he will help you.

- Isaiah 43:19 | I am about to do something new. See, I have already begun! Do you not see it? I will make a pathway through the wilderness. I will create rivers in the dry wasteland.

- Romans 5:18 | Yes, Adam's one sin brings condemnation for everyone, but Christ's one act of righteousness brings a right relationship with God and new life for everyone.

Maybe your dreams for your child or your family have been crushed. Maybe you realize that a dream you've been chasing will never happen. Many families have walked this road too. Let your broken heart be open to God. He alone has the ability to take your broken dreams and turn them into more than you ever hoped or imagined.

EMBARRASSMENT
When you feel embarrassed by your child's actions . . .

- Psalm 139:17 | How precious are your thoughts about me, O God. They cannot be numbered!

- PSALM 139:1-3, 6 | O LORD, you have examined my heart and know everything about me. You know when I sit down or stand up. You know my thoughts even when I'm far away. You see me when I travel and when I rest at home. You know everything I do. . . . Such knowledge is too wonderful for me, too great for me to understand!

- PHILIPPIANS 3:8 | Yes, everything else is worthless when compared with the infinite value of knowing Christ Jesus my Lord. For his sake I have discarded everything else, counting it all as garbage, so that I could gain Christ.

When you feel embarrassed that your child is different . . .

- GENESIS 1:27 | So God created human beings in his own image. In the image of God he created them; male and female he created them.

- GENESIS 1:26, 31 | Then God said, "Let us make human beings in our image, to be like us." . . . Then God looked over all he had made, and he saw that it was very good!

- PSALM 139:13-14 | You made all the delicate, inner parts of my body and knit me together in my mother's womb. Thank you for making me so wonderfully complex! Your workmanship is marvelous—how well I know it.

Wherever you go there may be people who don't understand your situation and will therefore judge you when your child acts differently from other children. It's natural to be embarrassed when that happens. But once you have collected yourself and have a moment to reflect, remind yourself that God made your child in his own image and that he loves him or her unconditionally. He is the only judge worth caring about, and his thoughts about your child are precious and loving, encouraging and comforting.

EMOTIONS

When you can't control your emotions . . .

- ROMANS 8:38 | Nothing can ever separate us from God's love.

- 1 JOHN 3:19-20 | Our actions will show that we belong to the truth, so we will be confident when we stand before God. Even if we feel guilty, God is greater than our feelings, and he knows everything.

- EZEKIEL 36:26 | I will give you a new heart, and I will put a new spirit in you. I will take out your stony, stubborn heart and give you a tender, responsive heart.

- GALATIANS 5:22-23 | The Holy Spirit produces this kind of fruit in our lives: love, joy, peace, patience, kindness, goodness, faithfulness, gentleness, and self-control. There is no law against these things!

When you wonder if God cares how you feel . . .

- MATTHEW 10:29; 31 | Not a single sparrow can fall to the ground without your Father knowing it. . . . So don't be afraid; you are more valuable to God than a whole flock of sparrows.

Parenting a child with special needs requires you to cope with a wide range of emotions—both yours and your child's. Emotions are a good gift from God. They are evidence that you are made in his image, for the Bible shows God displaying a whole range of emotions—from anger to zeal. But like any gift from God, emotions can be misused. Instead of being a blessing, they can become a curse. Emotions come from the heart, where there is a desperate battle going on between your old sinful nature and your new nature in Christ. This new nature Christ gives helps you use your emotions to reflect his character, which will help you love your family and others in healthy ways. You must learn to understand your emotions and direct them in ways that are productive and not destructive. The issue isn't the power or intensity of the emotion, but what it leads you to do.

ENCOURAGEMENT

When you need some encouragement to keep going . . .

- PSALM 138:3 | As soon as I pray, you answer me; you encourage me by giving me strength.

- ROMANS 15:4 | The Scriptures give us hope and encouragement as we wait patiently for God's promises to be fulfilled.

- 2 THESSALONIANS 2:16-17 | Now may our Lord Jesus Christ himself and God our Father, who loved us and by his grace gave us eternal comfort and a wonderful hope, comfort you and strengthen you in every good thing you do and say.

When you wonder how you can encourage other special needs families . . .

- HEBREWS 10:24 | Let us think of ways to motivate one another to acts of love and good works.

- ROMANS 15:2 | We should help others do what is right and build them up in the Lord.

- ROMANS 15:7 | Accept each other just as Christ has accepted you so that God will be given glory.

- 1 THESSALONIANS 5:11 | Encourage each other and build each other up, just as you are already doing.

- GALATIANS 6:2 | Share each other's burdens, and in this way obey the law of Christ.

Encouragers bring the beautiful gift of renewal. They help you regain commitment, resolve, and motivation. When you grow weary, when bills pile up, or when no progress seems evident despite your hard work, you need someone to remind you that joy is possible every day through Jesus Christ! Are there people in your life who can give you this kind of help? They will be such an inspiration to you. Maybe God is even nudging you to offer a hopeful perspective to other families who have children with special needs. Encouragers are an important part of your support group, but remember that God is always available when others cannot be. He understands your challenges and adversities better than anyone, and through his Word he offers constant encouragement. When you feel disheartened and need new courage to face what's ahead, first turn to the promises of God to be assured of his love and goodness to you and your child.

ENDURANCE

When you're tempted to give up or give in . . .

- GALATIANS 6:8-10 | Those who live only to satisfy their own sinful nature will harvest decay and death from that sinful nature. But those who live to please the Spirit will harvest everlasting life from the Spirit. So let's not get tired of doing what is good. At just the right time we will reap a harvest of blessing if we don't give up. Therefore, whenever we have the opportunity, we should do good to everyone—especially to those in the family of faith.

When you feel like you're fighting a losing battle . . .

- PSALM 125:1 | Those who trust in the LORD are as secure as Mount Zion; they will not be defeated but will endure forever.

When you walk in God's strength . . .

- PSALM 138:8 | The LORD will work out his plans for my life—for your faithful love, O LORD, endures forever.

- PHILIPPIANS 4:13 | I can do everything through Christ, who gives me strength.

Life is like a marathon. You need endurance to complete the journey well. And there are tangible rewards for finishing strong—an inheritance to pass along, a reputation others can follow, a legacy. You want to be a parent who goes the distance, but sometimes life pushes you to the limit of what you feel you can endure. Perhaps your child doesn't sleep and you don't know how to make it through another day, or maybe the challenges your child is facing pile so high that you feel like giving up. If you're struggling to keep going today, hold on to God's promises that you can endure through Christ who gives you strength!

ENERGY

When you need some energy and you wonder where it's going to come from . . .

- ISAIAH 40:28-31 | Have you never heard? Have you never understood? The LORD is the everlasting God, the Creator of all the earth. He never grows weak or weary. No one can measure the depths of his understanding. He gives power to the weak and strength to the powerless. Even youths will become weak and tired, and young men will fall in exhaustion. But those who trust in the LORD will find new strength. They will soar high on wings like eagles. They will run and not grow weary. They will walk and not faint.

- 1 PETER 4:10-11 | God has given each of you a gift from his great variety of spiritual gifts. Use them well to serve one another. Do you have the gift of speaking? Then speak as though God himself were speaking through you. Do you have the gift of helping others? Do it with all the strength and energy that God supplies. Then everything you do will bring glory to God through Jesus Christ.

- PSALM 73:26 | My health may fail, and my spirit may grow weak, but God remains the strength of my heart; he is mine forever.

When your child has endless energy and you're exhausted . . .

- PSALM 119:50 | Your promise revives me; it comforts me in all my troubles.

- PSALM 121:4; 124:8 | Indeed, he who watches over Israel never slumbers or sleeps. . . . Our help is from the LORD, who made heaven and earth.

Constantly meeting the needs of your child can be draining. Perhaps you wake up already empty and wonder how you will find the energy to get through the day. These verses don't promise instant physical revival, although nothing is impossible for God. However, God himself loves to provide power and strength to those who feel weak and worn out. If your child doesn't sleep well, it means you may not either. God is awake with you. He knows you need rest and refreshment. You have the Holy Spirit in you—the very power and strength of God. He promises you will find new strength as you trust him. Through his Spirit, God gives you the energy and the resources you need to care for yourself and your child.

❖

ESCAPE

When you want to run from your problems . . .

- NAHUM 1:7 | The LORD is good, a strong refuge when trouble comes. He is close to those who trust in him.

- PSALM 32:7 | You are my hiding place; you protect me from trouble. You surround me with songs of victory.

- EPHESIANS 6:10-11 | Be strong in the Lord and in his mighty power. Put on all of God's armor so that you will be able to stand firm against all strategies of the devil.

When you're tempted to use addictions as a form of escape . . .

- 2 PETER 1:3-4 | By his divine power, God has given us everything we need for living a godly life. We have received all of this by coming to know him, the one who called us to himself by means of his marvelous glory and excellence. And because of his glory and excellence, he has given us great and precious promises. These are the promises that enable you to share his divine nature and escape the world's corruption caused by human desires.

When the pressures of life become too much, it's easy to want to relieve the stress by escaping for a while. However, unresolved problems will follow you no matter where you go. There are many ways you can be tempted to escape your life—traveling, working too many hours, spending time on social media, or misusing food or alcohol. While it's important to give yourself some breaks, make sure your time away is not spent indulging in sin or destructive habits but is giving you the energy you need to jump back in and love your family well. Spending time with God is the perfect escape that can happen anytime, anywhere. A few moments in prayer or meditating on his Word can reenergize you with a fresh attitude and the perspective to face those tough situations in your life.

ETERNITY

When you wonder if there is life after death . . .

- ISAIAH 26:19 | Those who die in the LORD will live; their bodies will rise again! Those who sleep in the earth will rise up and sing for joy! For your life-giving light will fall like dew on your people in the place of the dead!

- JOHN 3:16 | This is how God loved the world: He gave his one and only Son, so that everyone who believes in him will not perish but have eternal life.

- 2 CORINTHIANS 5:1 | We know that when this earthly tent we live in is taken down (that is, when we die and leave this earthly body), we will have a house in heaven, an eternal body made for us by God himself and not by human hands.

When you want the certainty of eternity to change your perspective on today . . .

- ROMANS 8:28 | We know that God causes everything to work together for the good of those who love God and are called according to his purpose for them.

- 1 PETER 1:7 | These trials will show that your faith is genuine. It is being tested as fire tests and purifies gold—though your faith is far more precious than mere gold. So when your faith remains strong through many trials, it will bring you much praise and glory and honor on the day when Jesus Christ is revealed to the whole world.

- LUKE 18:27 | [Jesus] replied, "What is impossible for people is possible with God."

Like many parents of children with special needs, you may be operating in day-to-day survival mode; today is all you can think about. With survival mode often comes a sense of purposelessness or the feeling that life has been reduced to a to-do list. If you need a fresh outlook on your life and your situation, try taking the long view. Put your circumstances and worries under the lens of God's eternal love and promise of heaven. The problems you experience are discomforts, but they remind you that you and your child have not yet arrived at your true home in heaven where you will be at rest, your body will be fully healed, and you will enjoy unbroken relationships with God and others. When you look at your life with eternal perspective, your troubles transform into opportunities to experience the power and glory of the eternal God in the here and now.

EXPECTATIONS

When it hits you that your life isn't turning out the way you expected . . .

- ISAIAH 55:8 | "My thoughts are nothing like your thoughts," says the LORD. "And my ways are far beyond anything you could imagine."

- ROMANS 5:3-5 | We can rejoice, too, when we run into problems and trials, for we know that they help us develop endurance. And endurance develops strength of character, and character strengthens our confident hope of salvation. And this hope will not lead to disappointment. For we know how dearly God loves us, because he has given us the Holy Spirit to fill our hearts with his love.

When people don't live up to your expectations . . .

- EPHESIANS 4:32 | Be kind to each other, tenderhearted, forgiving one another, just as God through Christ has forgiven you.

- PSALM 145:8 | The LORD is merciful and compassionate, slow to get angry and filled with unfailing love.

- LAMENTATIONS 3:21-22 | I still dare to hope when I remember this: The faithful love of the LORD never ends! His mercies never cease.

When you wonder what you can expect in life . . .

- JOHN 16:33 | [Jesus said,] "Here on earth you will have many trials and sorrows. But take heart, because I have overcome the world. "

- 1 PETER 1:3-4 | All praise to God, the Father of our Lord Jesus Christ. It is by his great mercy that we have been born again, because God raised Jesus Christ from the dead. Now we live with great expectation, and we have a priceless inheritance—an inheritance that is kept in heaven for you, pure and undefiled, beyond the reach of change and decay.

An expectation is a strong hope or confidence that something will occur. Before you had children, you probably had a picture in your mind of how your family would look. When you discovered that your child has special needs, the reality of your family was probably a little different from what you pictured. How does this shape how you feel toward God? Do you find you are able to trust him, or do you feel that God has placed unrealistic expectations on you? Do you wonder how you can possibly accomplish all that is now expected of you and still love according to his standards? God's greatest expectation is not that you live a perfect life or accomplish everything you think you have to—that is humanly impossible. It is simply that you love him with all your heart. Understanding that God doesn't expect you to do it all, but rather applauds you when you sincerely try to follow him, can be a divine moment where you no longer see him as a strict taskmaster but as a loving encourager who strengthens you to joyfully love and embrace life, even when it doesn't turn out the way you expected.

FAITH

When you need faith that moves mountains . . .

- MATTHEW 21:21-22 | Jesus told them, "I tell you the truth, if you have faith and don't doubt, you can do things like this and much more. You can even say to this mountain, 'May you be lifted up and thrown into the sea,' and it will happen. You can pray for anything, and if you have faith, you will receive it."

When you stumble during trials . . .

- 1 PETER 1:7 | These trials will show that your faith is genuine. It is being tested as fire tests and purifies gold— though your faith is far more precious than mere gold. So when your faith remains strong through many trials, it will bring you much praise and glory and honor on the day when Jesus Christ is revealed to the whole world.

- ISAIAH 26:3 | You will keep in perfect peace all who trust in you, all whose thoughts are fixed on you!

- 1 JOHN 5:4 | For every child of God defeats this evil world, and we achieve this victory through our faith.

When you need faith that keeps you going . . .

- HEBREWS 11:1 | Faith shows the reality of what we hope for; it is the evidence of things we cannot see.

When you let Jesus lead you . . .

- MARK 5:36 | [Jesus said,] "Don't be afraid. Just have faith."

- JOHN 5:24 | [Jesus said,] "I tell you the truth, those who listen to my message and believe in God who sent me have eternal life. They will never be condemned . . . they have already passed from death into life."

The obstacles you face as a special needs parent are opportunities for your faith to grow. Having faith means that you choose to trust that God is who he says he is in the Bible and that he will do what he has promised. Faith is more than just believing; it is trusting your very life to what you believe. It means moving forward—perhaps without answers—with the assurance that God is with you and that he will guide you. Faith is an act of surrender, a willingness to keep yourself focused on God and his ways even when they don't seem to make sense. When life seems crazy, you can be absolutely confident that one day Jesus will come and make it right again. Your faith in his promises will allow you to keep going today.

FAMILY

When you wonder if God can use your imperfect family . . .

- PSALM 68:5-6 | Father to the fatherless, defender of widows—this is God, whose dwelling is holy. God places the lonely in families; he sets the prisoners free and gives them joy.

- 2 TIMOTHY 2:21 | If you keep yourself pure, you will be a special utensil for honorable use. Your life will be clean, and you will be ready for the Master to use you for every good work.

- HEBREWS 12:12-13 | Take a new grip with your tired hands and strengthen your weak knees. Mark out a straight path for your feet so that those who are weak and lame will not fall but become strong.

When your family doesn't understand your child's needs . . .

- HEBREWS 4:15-16 | This High Priest of ours understands our weaknesses, for he faced all of the same testings we do, yet he did not sin. So let us come boldly to the throne of our gracious God. There we will receive his mercy, and we will find grace to help us when we need it most.

When others judge your family . . .

- PSALM 58:11 | Then at last everyone will say, "There truly is a reward for those who live for God; surely there is a God who judges justly here on earth."

When you want to leave a legacy . . .

- PSALM 127:1-5 | Unless the LORD builds a house, the work of the builders is wasted. Unless the LORD protects a city, guarding it with sentries will do no good. It is useless for you to work so hard from early morning until late at night, anxiously working for food to eat; for God gives rest to his loved ones. Children are a gift from the LORD; they are a reward from him. Children born to a young man are like arrows in a warrior's hands. How joyful is the man whose quiver is full of them!

- 1 CORINTHIANS 3:10-11 | Because of God's grace to me, I have laid the foundation like an expert builder. Now others are building on it. But whoever is building on this foundation must be very careful. For no one can lay any foundation other than the one we already have—Jesus Christ.

Your child's needs and the messiness of your family don't exclude you from God's glorious plans. Although it may not feel like you're living them out day-to-day, you are building a legacy. When friends and family don't understand you or when others judge, remember that Jesus understands and invites you to come to him for mercy and grace. Build your family around the Lord. Invite him into your daily routine, and ask him to use you as you care for your child. He wants to be the source of your family's joy and comfort. In this way, you will be building a legacy of faith, and your family will bless others by how you live.

FEAR

When you need courage to face a new obstacle . . .

- 2 TIMOTHY 1:7 | God has not given us a spirit of fear and timidity, but of power, love, and self-discipline.

- PSALM 46:1-2 | God is our refuge and strength, always ready to help in times of trouble. So we will not fear when earthquakes come and the mountains crumble into the sea.

When you're drowning in the storm . . .

- PSALM 29:10-11 | The LORD rules over the floodwaters. The LORD reigns as king forever. The LORD gives his people strength. The LORD blesses them with peace.

When others don't value your child and you're afraid no one cares . . .

- LUKE 12:6-7 | What is the price of five sparrows— two copper coins? Yet God does not forget a single one of them. And the very hairs on your head are all numbered. So don't be afraid; you are more valuable to God than a whole flock of sparrows.

- PSALM 139:17-18 | How precious are your thoughts about me, O God. They cannot be numbered! I can't even count them.

Having a child with special needs presents many opportunities for fear—fear that your child's development isn't quite right or maybe even fear for his health or life. Whenever fear sweeps over you, train yourself to remember God's promises. God lives in you, and his presence with you offers you power, love, and a sound mind. He is sovereign over all circumstances. There is nothing you encounter that God cannot handle. You and your child are precious to him. Let these truths calm your heart and bring you renewed courage in moments of worry and crisis.

FINANCES
When the bills pile up . . .

- PSALM 34:9 | Fear the LORD, you his godly people, for those who fear him will have all they need.

- MATTHEW 6:31-33 | [Jesus said,] "So don't worry about these things, saying, 'What will we eat? What will we drink? What will we wear?' These things dominate the thoughts of unbelievers, but your heavenly Father already knows all your needs. Seek the Kingdom of God above all else, and live righteously, and he will give you everything you need."

When worries about money fill your thoughts . . .

- JOHN 1:16 | From his abundance we have all received one gracious blessing after another.

- ROMANS 8:31-32 | What shall we say about such wonderful things as these? If God is for us, who can ever be against us? Since he did not spare even his own Son but gave him up for us all, won't he also give us everything else?

When money is where you find your security . . .

- PROVERBS 11:28 | Trust in your money and down you go! But the godly flourish like leaves in spring.

- MATTHEW 6:19-21 | [Jesus said,] "Don't store up treasures here on earth, where moths eat them and rust destroys them, and where thieves break in and steal. Store your treasures in heaven, where moths and rust cannot destroy, and thieves do not break in and steal. Wherever your treasure is, there the desires of your heart will also be."

- PROVERBS 30:7-9 | O God . . . give me neither poverty nor riches! Give me just enough to satisfy my needs. For if I grow rich, I may deny you and say, "Who is the LORD?"

In times of financial crisis, money can dominate your thoughts. Trusting in your savings or in your income may bring security for a time, but it is a false sense of security. You have a heavenly Father who knows your needs and has the unlimited resources to help you. His help might not always come through money—it might come in the form of a neighbor's helping hand or volunteers from church. But you can trust in God's generous nature. Don't let the fear of financial distress rule your thoughts. Find your security in his loving presence, and desire him above all.

FORGIVENESS

When someone hurts your child and you're having a hard time forgiving . . .

- 1 PETER 3:8-9 | All of you should be of one mind. Sympathize with each other. Love each other as brothers and sisters. Be tenderhearted, and keep a humble attitude. Don't repay evil for evil. Don't retaliate with insults when people insult you. Instead, pay them back with a blessing. That is what God has called you to do, and he will grant you his blessing.

When you condemn yourself because of your past mistakes . . .

- ISAIAH 1:18 | "Come now, let's settle this," says the LORD. "Though your sins are like scarlet, I will make them as white as snow. Though they are red like crimson, I will make them as white as wool."

- ROMANS 8:1 | Now there is no condemnation for those who belong to Christ Jesus.

When you wonder why forgiveness matters . . .

- MATTHEW 6:14-15 | [Jesus said,] "If you forgive those who sin against you, your heavenly Father will forgive you. But if you refuse to forgive others, your Father will not forgive your sins."

Forgiveness matters. When you've been wronged, your natural reaction is to keep score or to nurse the pain. However, this only imprisons your heart. Forgiveness acknowledges the pain, but it sets both you and the offender free from the bondage of anger and bitterness. Forgiveness opens the doors for God's blessing. When you're struggling with your own mistakes, it is also important to forgive yourself and remember that there is no condemnation because you belong to Christ. In life, you will be offended and hurt by people. But you can choose to embrace God's gift of forgiveness and move forward in freedom and experience the blessings of a peaceful heart and restored relationship.

FRIENDS

When you need a friend . . .

- PSALM 145:18 | The LORD is close to all who call on him, yes, to all who call on him in truth.

- JOHN 15:15 | I no longer call you slaves, because a master doesn't confide in his slaves. Now you are my friends, since I have told you everything the Father told me.

- PSALM 25:14 | The LORD is a friend to those who fear him.

When your friends don't understand your challenges . . .

- PSALM 33:13-15 | The LORD looks down from heaven and sees the whole human race. From his throne he observes all who live on the earth. He made their hearts, so he understands everything they do.

- PROVERBS 18:24 | There are "friends" who destroy each other, but a real friend sticks closer than a brother.

When a friend says something hurtful . . .

- PROVERBS 17:9 | Love prospers when a fault is forgiven, but dwelling on it separates close friends.

When your child has trouble making or keeping friends . . .

- PSALM 68:5-6 | Father to the fatherless, defender of widows—this is God, whose dwelling is holy. God places the lonely in families; he sets the prisoners free and gives them joy.

- ROMANS 5:11 | Now we can rejoice in our wonderful new relationship with God because our Lord Jesus Christ has made us friends of God.

Being a parent of a child with special needs can be lonely. When it's hard to find friends or your friends don't understand what your life is like, you can find comfort in your friendship with God, who knows you intimately and understands your heart. It can also be hard if your child struggles to make connections with others. Even if your child doesn't know how to find friends, the Lord knows how to befriend him or her. You and your child were made for relationship, and God promises to be close to all who call on him.

FRUSTRATION
When you become totally frustrated . . .

- JOSHUA 1:9 | Be strong and courageous! Do not be afraid or discouraged. For the LORD your God is with you wherever you go.

- PSALM 90:14 | Satisfy us each morning with your unfailing love, so we may sing for joy to the end of our lives.

When you get stuck and can't figure it out . . .

- PSALM 16:11 | You will show me the way of life, granting me the joy of your presence and the pleasures of living with you forever.

- ISAIAH 43:16 | I am the LORD, who opened a way through the waters, making a dry path through the sea.

Is there a situation in your life or your child's life that makes you feel stuck? Perhaps you've been toilet training for years and you wonder if your child will ever learn. Or maybe there's a health issue that you just can't seem to resolve or an insurance issue that won't go away. Lack of progress or frequent encounters with uncomfortable or annoying circumstances can lead you to feel frustrated. Frustration can be expected, but it is temporary. The best way through it is to persevere. Don't let your frustration limit God's work in your life. Ask him to work through your challenges to accomplish great things.

FUN

When there's no time for fun . . .

- PSALM 16:8-9 | I know the LORD is always with me.
  I will not be shaken, for he is right beside me. No
  wonder my heart is glad, and I rejoice.

When you have something to celebrate . . .

- NEHEMIAH 8:10 | Go and celebrate with a feast of rich
  foods and sweet drinks, and share gifts of food with
  people who have nothing prepared. This is a sacred day
  before our Lord. Don't be dejected and sad, for the joy
  of the LORD is your strength!

When it's hard to relax . . .

- PSALM 5:11-12 | Let all who take refuge in you rejoice;
  let them sing joyful praises forever. Spread your protection over them, that all who love your name may be
  filled with joy. For you bless the godly, O LORD; you
  surround them with your shield of love.

When you long to have fun as a family . . .

- DEUTERONOMY 12:7 | There you and your families will
  feast in the presence of the LORD your God, and you
  will rejoice in all you have accomplished because the
  LORD your God has blessed you.

As a parent of a child with special needs you may frequently deal with serious issues. It is important to balance these responsibilities with times of rest and enjoyment. God commanded the Israelites to enjoy times of feasting as reminders of his provision and love for them. Sometimes you need to take a step back from the seriousness of life and look for reasons to celebrate. Your festivities don't have to be fancy; they could be as simple as having a picnic at a park or playing some happy music. Reflect on all God has done and find that the joy of the Lord really is a source of strength. This is a gift you can give to yourself and your family—a joyful celebration!

FUTURE
When you need hope for the future . . .

- 1 PETER 1:6 | Be truly glad. There is wonderful joy ahead, even though you must endure many trials for a little while.

- 1 PETER 1:4-5 | We have a priceless inheritance—an inheritance that is kept in heaven for you, pure and undefiled, beyond the reach of change and decay. And through your faith, God is protecting you by his power until you receive this salvation, which is ready to be revealed on the last day for all to see.

When the future seems uncertain . . .

- PSALM 32:8 | The LORD says, "I will guide you along the best pathway for your life. I will advise you and watch over you."

- PSALM 121:8 | The LORD keeps watch over you as you come and go, both now and forever.

When you feel you can't move forward . . .

- PSALM 139:5 | You go before me and follow me. You place your hand of blessing on my head.

When things are changing . . .

- HEBREWS 13:8 | Jesus Christ is the same yesterday, today, and forever.

When you worry about your child's future . . .

- PROVERBS 22:6 | Direct your children onto the right path, and when they are older, they will not leave it.

- DEUTERONOMY 11:18-19 | Commit yourselves whole-heartedly to these words of mine. Tie them to your hands and wear them on your forehead as reminders. Teach them to your children. Talk about them when you are at home and when you are on the road, when you are going to bed and when you are getting up.

- PSALM 68:19 | Praise the Lord; praise God our savior! For each day he carries us in his arms.

When you realize the future you planned might not happen . . .

- PSALM 31:14-15 | I am trusting you, O LORD, saying, "You are my God!" My future is in your hands.

- 1 CORINTHIANS 2:9 | That is what the Scriptures mean when they say, "No eye has seen, no ear has heard, and no mind has imagined what God has prepared for those who love him."

- PROVERBS 20:24 | The LORD directs our steps, so why try to understand everything along the way?

From where you stand right now, the future may seem scary. Feeling this way can make you doubt God's care for you and your family. Although the path you are on may lead through some dark valleys or take some puzzling detours, someday you will look back and discover that God's way for you and your child was the right way. When the future looks hopeless, remind yourself of times in the past when God went before you and prepared wonderful things you couldn't have anticipated. When you remember God's track record, you gain confidence for your future. God loves you and your child so much—why would he hold anything back? Cling to this hope for the future and wait expectantly for him to guide your next steps. And always remember that ultimately, all those who believe in Jesus Christ as their Lord and Savior will experience a perfect future for eternity!

GENEROSITY

When you need to reflect on God's generosity to you . . .

- TITUS 3:6 | He generously poured out the Spirit upon us through Jesus Christ our Savior.

- ROMANS 5:15 | There is a great difference between Adam's sin and God's gracious gift. For the sin of this one man, Adam, brought death to many. But even greater is God's wonderful grace and his gift of forgiveness to many through this other man, Jesus Christ.

- 1 CORINTHIANS 12:7, 11, 18 | A spiritual gift is given to each of us so we can help each other. . . . It is the one and only Spirit who distributes all these gifts. He alone decides which gift each person should have . . . and God has put each part just where he wants it.

- JOHN 3:16 | This is how God loved the world: He gave his one and only Son, so that everyone who believes in him will not perish but have eternal life.

When you're feeling tightfisted . . .

- ACTS 20:35 | It is more blessed to give than to receive.

- 2 CORINTHIANS 9:11-14 | Yes, you will be enriched in every way so that you can always be generous. And when we take your gifts to those who need them, they will thank God. So two good things will result from this ministry of giving—the needs of the believers . . . will be met, and they will joyfully express their thanks to God. As a result of your ministry [of giving], they will give glory to God. For your generosity to them . . . will prove that you are obedient to the Good News of Christ. And they will pray for you with deep affection because of the overflowing grace God has given to you.

- PROVERBS 11:25 | The generous will prosper; those who refresh others will themselves be refreshed.

When you wonder why you should go above and beyond . . .

- 2 CORINTHIANS 9:7-8 | You must each decide in your heart how much to give. And don't give reluctantly or in response to pressure. "For God loves a person who gives cheerfully." And God will generously provide all you need. Then you will always have everything you need and plenty left over to share with others.

When your emotional and physical resources are already stretched, it can be hard to feel generous. In fact, you may even feel you deserve something extra for the effort and resources you invest in caring for your child. At the core of our sinful human nature is the desire to get, not give; to accumulate, not relinquish; to look out for ourselves, not others. But God is calling you to practice radical generosity—in whatever way he shows you. This can mean investments of your resources, love, time, talents, money, or faith. You may feel like you have already given everything you have to help care for your child, but God has more in store for you both. God's resources never run out, and you can be his vehicle to bless others. It will involve sacrifice, but realizing that all you have is a gift from your generous God can motivate you to share your gifts and earthly possessions freely. The Bible promises that those who share generously will discover that the benefits of giving are far greater than anything we can imagine.

GLORY

When you wonder how God can be glorified through your child's special needs . . .

- PSALM 40:1, 3 | I waited patiently for the LORD to help me, and he turned to me and heard my cry. . . . He has given me a new song to sing. . . . Many will see what he has done and be amazed. They will put their trust in the LORD.

- PSALM 50:14-15 | Make thankfulness your sacrifice to God, and keep the vows you made to the Most High. Then call on me when you are in trouble, and I will rescue you, and you will give me glory.

- PSALM 111:2-3 | How amazing are the deeds of the LORD! All who delight in him should ponder them. Everything he does reveals his glory and majesty. His righteousness never fails.

When you desire God's glory to be seen through you . . .

- PSALM 71:7-8 | My life is an example to many, because you have been my strength and protection. That is why I can never stop praising you; I declare your glory all day long.

- ROMANS 5:3-5 | We can rejoice, too, when we run into problems and trials, for we know that they help us develop endurance. And endurance develops strength of character, and character strengthens our confident hope of salvation. And this hope will not lead to disappointment.

When you need to see more of God's glory . . .

- ROMANS 8:18, 22-24 | What we suffer now is nothing compared to the glory he will reveal to us later. . . .

For we know that all creation has been groaning as in the pains of childbirth right up to the present time. And we believers also groan, even though we have the Holy Spirit within us as a foretaste of future glory, for we long for our bodies to be released from sin and suffering. We, too, wait with eager hope for the day when God will give us our full rights as his adopted children, including the new bodies he has promised us. We were given this hope when we were saved.

- ROMANS 6:13 | Give yourselves completely to God. . . . Use your whole body as an instrument to do what is right for the glory of God.

- JOHN 15:8 | [Jesus said,] "When you produce much fruit, you are my true disciples. This brings great glory to my Father."

Everything God does reveals his glory, and he wants to reveal some of his glory through you and your child. Your weak moments, your less-than-perfect moments—these are opportunities for God's strength and power to be seen most clearly. When you think you have it all together, you aren't allowing God's power and strength to work through you and empower you beyond your abilities. He is glorified when you allow him to work through you to overcome great obstacles. You may look at your life right now and think it looks broken. Thank God for the brokenness and ask him to do his amazing work through it.

GOALS

When you need perspective on your ultimate goals . . .

- PSALM 40:8 | I take joy in doing your will, my God, for your instructions are written on my heart.

- PROVERBS 4:25-27 | Look straight ahead, and fix your eyes on what lies before you. Mark out a straight path for your feet; stay on the safe path. Don't get sidetracked; keep your feet from following evil.

- PHILIPPIANS 3:13-14 | I focus on this one thing: Forgetting the past and looking forward to what lies ahead, I press on to reach the end of the race and receive the heavenly prize for which God, through Christ Jesus, is calling us.

When you wonder if your child will meet the goals you're working toward . . .

- ZECHARIAH 4:10 | Do not despise these small beginnings, for the LORD rejoices to see the work begin.

- GALATIANS 6:9 | Let's not get tired of doing what is good. At just the right time we will reap a harvest of blessing if we don't give up.

When you wonder what kind of goals to set . . .

- 1 CORINTHIANS 14:1 | Let love be your highest goal!

- MICAH 6:8 | The LORD has told you what is good, and this is what he requires of you: to do what is right, to love mercy, and to walk humbly with your God.

- LUKE 12:31 | Seek the Kingdom of God above all else, and he will give you everything you need.

Goals are necessary for staying on track. In therapy, you set goals for your child's physical or behavioral development. In a medical setting, you set goals for improving your child's health. At school you might set goals as part of your child's educational plan. By planning ahead and setting attainable goals, the therapist or doctor ensures that your child will stay on the right track and arrive at a particular point of health or development. The same principle is true for you. Setting attainable goals gives you a destination and the direction to get there. Without goals, it is easy to wander from what you value. But the key is setting *attainable* goals. When you set unrealistic goals, you will be discouraged when you don't reach them and may feel like giving up. It's okay to take baby steps. Most people make progress one step at a time. When setting goals, invite God to inspire each step you take. Allow him to write a life plan for you and your child. He may surprise you along the way, but you can walk with confidence that he is leading you both in the best direction.

GOD'S TIMING

When you're tired of waiting . . .

- JEREMIAH 29:11 | "For I know the plans I have for you," says the LORD. "They are plans for good and not for disaster, to give you a future and a hope."

- PSALM 138:8 | The LORD will work out his plans for my life—for your faithful love, O LORD, endures forever. Don't abandon me, for you made me.

- ISAIAH 40:31 | Those who trust in the LORD will find new strength. They will soar high on wings like eagles. They will run and not grow weary. They will walk and not faint.

When turbulent times make you long for God's justice . . .

- PSALM 75:2-3 | God says, "At the time I have planned, I will bring justice against the wicked. When the earth quakes and its people live in turmoil, I am the one who keeps its foundations firm."

- EPHESIANS 1:9-10 | God has now revealed to us his mysterious will regarding Christ—which is to fulfill his own good plan. And this is the plan: At the right time he will bring everything together under the authority of Christ—everything in heaven and on earth.

Whether it's the fast pace of the world today or because you can't see the whole scope of your life, it is easy to become impatient when you're waiting for something. The key to a peaceful heart in times of waiting is trusting God's promise that he has a plan for your life and is working out that plan for you. God's love is forever, and his plans are for good. He wants you to have hope. At the right time, everything will be made perfect under the authority of Jesus Christ.

GRACE
When it's hard to remember what God has done for you . . .

- EPHESIANS 2:10 | We are God's masterpiece. He has created us anew in Christ Jesus, so we can do the good things he planned for us long ago.

- TITUS 3:7 | Because of his grace he made us right in his sight and gave us confidence that we will inherit eternal life.

- EPHESIANS 1:6-8 | We praise God for the glorious grace he has poured out on us who belong to his dear Son. He is so rich in kindness and grace that he purchased our freedom with the blood of his Son and forgave our sins. He has showered his kindness on us, along with all wisdom and understanding.

When you wonder if God's grace is enough . . .

- ACTS 20:32 | Now I entrust you to God and the message of his grace that is able to build you up and give you an inheritance with all those he has set apart for himself.

- ROMANS 5:17 | The sin of this one man, Adam, caused death to rule over many. But even greater is God's wonderful grace and his gift of righteousness, for all who receive it will live in triumph over sin and death through this one man, Jesus Christ.

- PHILIPPIANS 1:6 | I am certain that God, who began the good work within you, will continue his work until it is finally finished on the day when Christ Jesus returns.

Because of grace, we receive what we don't deserve and escape many of the consequences we do deserve. God's ultimate act of grace—giving us eternal life with him instead of eternal death—is an example of how we are to extend grace to others. We are to be quick to forgive, hasty to extend kindness, and generous in love—even when others don't deserve it. Grace is one of the most tangible expressions of love. So let God's unfailing grace motivate you to pour out grace on your child and others in your life. Ask God to increase your understanding of his grace so you will be moved to share that same gift with those around you, and pray that he will develop a spirit of graciousness and mercy in you that consistently spills into the lives of others, so they, too, might be blessed by his special favor.

GRIEF
When you wonder if God knows your grief . . .

- JOHN 11:35 | Then Jesus wept.

- PSALM 116:15 | The LORD cares deeply when his loved ones die.

- ISAIAH 51:12 | I, yes I, am the one who comforts you.

- PSALM 10:17 | LORD, you know the hopes of the help-
  less. Surely you will hear their cries and comfort them.

- PSALM 31:7 | I will be glad and rejoice in your unfailing
  love, for you have seen my troubles, and you care about
  the anguish of my soul.

When the pain is still fresh in your mind . . .

- LAMENTATIONS 3:20-23 | I will never forget this awful
  time, as I grieve over my loss. Yet I still dare to hope
  when I remember this: The faithful love of the LORD
  never ends! His mercies never cease. Great is his faithfulness; his mercies begin afresh each morning.

When you can't find the words to express your pain . . .

- ROMANS 8:26-27 | The Holy Spirit helps us in our
  weakness. For example, we don't know what God wants
  us to pray for. But the Holy Spirit prays for us with
  groanings that cannot be expressed in words. And the
  Father who knows all hearts knows what the Spirit is
  saying, for the Spirit pleads for us believers in harmony
  with God's own will.

When your sorrows leave you feeling weary . . .

- PSALM 73:26 | My health may fail, and my spirit may
  grow weak, but God remains the strength of my heart;
  he is mine forever.

- MATTHEW 5:4 | God blesses those who mourn, for they will be comforted.

Grief is overwhelming sadness. In the moment, it feels like the pain will never end. In times of grief it is okay to cry, wail, and weep. God promises that the Holy Spirit will help you express the pain in your heart. God cares deeply, and he offers you his comfort. When you are weak with grief, God remains strong. He stands by you through tears and laughter, joy and sorrow. Lean on God. His faithfulness can be trusted, and he gives new mercies every day.

GUIDANCE

When you wish Jesus would point out the way to go . . .

- JOHN 14:6-7 | Jesus told him, "I am the way, the truth, and the life. No one can come to the Father except through me. If you had really known me, you would know who my Father is. From now on, you do know him and have seen him!"

When you want to do what honors the Lord . . .

- PSALM 119:11 | I have hidden your word in my heart, that I might not sin against you.

- PSALM 143:10 | Teach me to do your will, for you are my God. May your gracious Spirit lead me forward on a firm footing.

When your life is going in a direction you wouldn't choose . . .

- PROVERBS 3:5-6 | Trust in the LORD with all your heart; do not depend on your own understanding. Seek his will in all you do, and he will show you which path to take.

When things are confusing and you need discernment . . .

- PSALM 119:31-32 | I cling to your laws. LORD, don't let me be put to shame! I will pursue your commands, for you expand my understanding.

- PSALM 73:24 | You guide me with your counsel, leading me to a glorious destiny.

Do you ever wish your child's diagnosis came with a guidebook to help you navigate through the situations and seasons of special needs parenting? When you need some direction, remember God's Word. Knowing Scripture helps you make decisions in line with God's will and move forward in ways that please him. The Bible is full of good counsel for living, but even more, it gives language to the Holy Spirit's work in your life, expanding your understanding and leading forward in glorious ways. When you don't know the way ahead, remember that Jesus is the way. Wherever he is, that is where you want to follow. In everything you do, depend on God and trust in him more than in your own understanding, and he will make your path straight.

GUILT

When you wonder if you're to blame for your circumstances . . .

- HEBREWS 10:22 | Let us go right into the presence of God with sincere hearts fully trusting him. For our guilty consciences have been sprinkled with Christ's blood to make us clean, and our bodies have been washed with pure water.

- ROMANS 3:23-24 | Everyone has sinned; we all fall short of God's glorious standard. Yet God, in his grace, freely makes us right in his sight. He did this through Christ Jesus when he freed us from the penalty for our sins.

When you feel guilty for having lost your temper with your child . . .

- PSALM 103:8-10 | The LORD is compassionate and merciful, slow to get angry and filled with unfailing love. He will not constantly accuse us, nor remain angry forever. He does not punish us for all our sins; he does not deal harshly with us, as we deserve.

- PSALM 119:132 | Come and show me your mercy, as you do for all who love your name.

- 1 PETER 2:10 | Once you received no mercy; now you have received God's mercy.

The voice of guilt condemns you, blames you, and makes you a slave to fear. Grace is the antidote to guilt. God's grace is an invitation to give the burden of guilt to him and walk forward in transformation and freedom. When the world points its finger of blame at you or when you lose control of your emotions and do something you regret, that is the moment to go to God to exchange the guilt that haunts you for his grace that gives you hope.

HEALING

When you're praying for a full recovery for your child . . .

- PSALM 55:17 | Morning, noon, and night I cry out in my distress, and the LORD hears my voice.

- PSALM 103:3-5 | He forgives all my sins and heals all my diseases. He redeems me from death and crowns me with love and tender mercies. He fills my life with good things. My youth is renewed like the eagle's!

When you need God to mend your broken spirit . . .

- MALACHI 4:2 | For you who fear my name, the Sun of Righteousness will rise with healing in his wings. And you will go free, leaping with joy like calves let out to pasture.

- PSALM 116:7-8 | Let my soul be at rest again, for the LORD has been good to me. He has saved me from death, my eyes from tears, my feet from stumbling.

When your child is sick, your heart is breaking, or you wish that your child's special needs would disappear, these are the moments you long for healing. Take that longing to God. Cry out to him. He promises he is listening. Healing is a process, and waiting for it can make you restless. Turn your thoughts to the good things God has already done to boost your confidence in his care for you and your family. For reasons beyond your understanding, he might allow for your child not to be healed in this life, but you can be absolutely assured that when Jesus returns to renew all things, your child will be fully healthy for all eternity. Stop for a moment and let your mind picture what that will look like.

HEALTH

When sickness seems to follow your family everywhere . . .

- ISAIAH 58:11 | The LORD will guide you continually, giving you water when you are dry and restoring your strength. You will be like a well-watered garden, like an ever-flowing spring.

- 1 CORINTHIANS 15:43 | Our bodies are buried in brokenness, but they will be raised in glory. They are buried in weakness, but they will be raised in strength.

When you want to make healthier choices . . .

- PROVERBS 16:24 | Kind words are like honey—sweet to the soul and healthy for the body.

- PROVERBS 17:22 | A cheerful heart is good medicine, but a broken spirit saps a person's strength.

- PSALM 119:93 | I will never forget your commandments, for by them you give me life.

When you want to be spiritually fit . . .

- 1 TIMOTHY 4:8 | Physical training is good, but training for godliness is much better, promising benefits in this life and in the life to come.

- ISAIAH 38:16 | Lord, your discipline is good, for it leads to life and health. You restore my health and allow me to live!

The healthiest way to live isn't by following a diet, exercise, or supplement regimen. The healthiest way to live is by following God's Word. The Bible shows you and your family how to break free from the stress, pressure, and unhealthy practices that undermine your health, be it physical, mental, emotional, moral, or spiritual. Whether you and your child have good health or poor health, you must rely on God for strength of spirit. Whether or not God chooses to provide healing, you can experience a vibrant life through knowing him personally and walking with him daily.

HEAVEN

When you want to encourage your child with the hope of heaven . . .

- JOHN 3:16 | This is how God loved the world: He gave his one and only Son, so that everyone who believes in him will not perish but have eternal life.

- ACTS 16:31 | Believe in the Lord Jesus and you will be saved.

When you wonder if you will go to heaven . . .

- ROMANS 10:9-10 | If you openly declare that Jesus is Lord and believe in your heart that God raised him from the dead, you will be saved. For it is by believing in your heart that you are made right with God, and it is by openly declaring your faith that you are saved.

- ROMANS 3:22 | We are made right with God by placing our faith in Jesus Christ. And this is true for everyone who believes, no matter who we are.

When the pain of this life makes you long for heaven . . .

- 2 PETER 3:13 | We are looking forward to the new heavens and new earth he has promised, a world filled with God's righteousness.

- PHILIPPIANS 3:20-21 | We are citizens of heaven, where the Lord Jesus Christ lives. And we are eagerly waiting for him to return as our Savior. He will take our weak mortal bodies and change them into glorious bodies like his own, using the same power with which he will bring everything under his control.

When this life seems too short . . .

- 1 JOHN 2:17 | This world is fading away, along with everything that people crave. But anyone who does what pleases God will live forever.

- PSALM 39:4-5, 7 | LORD, remind me how brief my time on earth will be. Remind me that my days are numbered—how fleeting my life is. You have made my life no longer than the width of my hand. My entire lifetime is just a moment to you; at best, each of us is but a breath. . . . And so, Lord, where do I put my hope? My only hope is in you.

Feeling disappointment with this world isn't meant to lead you to feelings of hopelessness. It is meant to grow your hope and desire for heaven. Things in this world aren't as they should be. Our bodies and minds don't always work correctly, and we struggle with faith and relationships. God promises that in heaven everything will be made right again, as it was when he first created the world. Does that sound too good to be true? It's actually too good to miss!

Your life on this earth will fade away, but if you believe in the eternal God, you will not pass away forgotten. Your longing for something more is your built-in desire for an unbroken relationship with God. If you confess Jesus as the Son of God and believe this in your heart, God opens the way to eternal life in a place called heaven where you will experience the perfect home he has prepared just for you.

HELP

When your burdens are too heavy to carry . . .

- 1 PETER 5:7 | Give all your worries and cares to God, for he cares about you.

- MATTHEW 11:28-29 | Jesus said, "Come to me, all of you who are weary and carry heavy burdens, and I will give you rest. Take my yoke upon you. Let me teach you, because I am humble and gentle at heart, and you will find rest for your souls."

When you need help but can't ask for it . . .

- JAMES 1:5 | If you need wisdom, ask our generous God, and he will give it to you. He will not rebuke you for asking.

When you're feeling desperate . . .

- PSALM 40:17 | As for me, since I am poor and needy, let the Lord keep me in his thoughts. You are my helper and my savior. O my God, do not delay.

- PSALM 66:5-6 | Come and see what our God has done, what awesome miracles he performs for people! He made a dry path through the Red Sea, and his people went across on foot.

When others hurt more than they help . . .

- HEBREWS 13:6 | We can say with confidence, "The LORD is my helper, so I will have no fear. What can mere people do to me?"

- PSALM 121:1-2, 8 | I look up to the mountains—does my help come from there? My help comes from the LORD, who made heaven and earth! . . . The LORD keeps watch over you as you come and go, both now and forever.

It is comforting to think that God's goodness and love are always pursuing you. Whether you've lost the help you've had, or you're in desperate need for new help as you care for your child and handle other responsibilities, God walks with you and is ready to lift the burdens from your shoulders into his capable hands. God wants you to know him as Helper and Savior. He is the one who made a road through the sea so his people could walk forward in safety. With God, you are never without help!

HOPE

When you're looking for hope . . .

- 2 CORINTHIANS 4:8-10 | We are pressed on every side by troubles, but we are not crushed. We are perplexed, but not driven to despair. . . . We get knocked down, but we are not destroyed. Through suffering, our bodies continue to share in the death of Jesus so that the life of Jesus may also be seen in our bodies.

- 2 CORINTHIANS 4:17 | Our present troubles are small and won't last very long. Yet they produce for us a glory that vastly outweighs them and will last forever!

When your situation seems hopeless . . .

- PSALM 10:17 | LORD, you know the hopes of the helpless. Surely you will hear their cries and comfort them.

- ROMANS 5:6 | When we were utterly helpless, Christ came at just the right time and died for us sinners.

- PSALM 18:4-6 | The ropes of death entangled me; floods of destruction swept over me. The grave wrapped its ropes around me; death laid a trap in my path. But in my distress I cried out to the LORD; yes, I prayed to my God for help. He heard me from his sanctuary; my cry to him reached his ears.

When you feel hopeful about God's plans for your family . . .

- PROVERBS 10:28-29 | The hopes of the godly result in happiness, but the expectations of the wicked come to nothing. The way of the LORD is a stronghold to those with integrity.

- PSALM 25:4-5 | Show me the right path, O LORD; point out the road for me to follow. Lead me by your truth and teach me, for you are the God who saves me. All day long I put my hope in you.

When you've just received a hard diagnosis or realized that a dream of yours won't come true, you may feel hopeless, like you're drowning in emotional pain or stumbling around in darkness. But you are not lost to God. He knows what you long for, and he knows your needs as well as your child's. He wants to be a part of the process of creating new dreams with you. Cry out to him and share your heart. Ask him to give you a new dream for you and your family. Hope gives you the strength to endure many hard circumstances. When it gets dark, place your hope in the true light that can illuminate new dreams in your life. God promises to bring good from adversity when you place your hope in his unfailing love.

HURT

When you feel betrayed . . .

- ROMANS 3:3-4 | True, some of them were unfaithful; but just because they were unfaithful, does that mean God will be unfaithful? Of course not! Even if everyone else is a liar, God is true.

- ISAIAH 54:10 | "For the mountains may move and the hills disappear, but even then my faithful love for you will remain. My covenant of blessing will never be broken," says the LORD, who has mercy on you.

When your heart just aches . . .

- 2 CORINTHIANS 1:3 | All praise to God, the Father of our Lord Jesus Christ. God is our merciful Father and the source of all comfort.

- PSALM 31:7 | I will be glad and rejoice in your unfailing love, for you have seen my troubles, and you care about the anguish of my soul.

- PSALM 34:18 | The LORD is close to the brokenhearted; he rescues those whose spirits are crushed.

Sometimes you hurt because of present circumstances—like watching your child struggle in school or undergo intense medical interventions. Much of your hurt can also come from relationships with those around you. When your heart has been broken, it may respond defensively by pushing others away, including God. When wrestling with daily hurts, embrace God, who will carry you through. When you want to push him away, remember who he is: He is true, his love never fails, he is your source of comfort, he cares about your heartache, he is close, and he is your rescuer. When you are hurt by a friend, loved one, or even tough circumstances, it is a reminder that you long for a more perfect relationship with the One who will never hurt or disappoint you.

IMPOSSIBLE

When you wonder if a typical life will be possible . . .

- PSALM 39:7 | Lord, where do I put my hope? My only hope is in you.

- 1 CHRONICLES 28:20 | Be strong and courageous, and do the work. Don't be afraid or discouraged, for the

LORD God, my God, is with you. He will not fail you or forsake you.

- ROMANS 11:33-36 | Oh, how great are God's riches and wisdom and knowledge! How impossible it is for us to understand his decisions and his ways! For who can know the LORD's thoughts? Who knows enough to give him advice? And who has given him so much that he needs to pay it back? For everything comes from him and exists by his power and is intended for his glory. All glory to him forever! Amen.

- PHILIPPIANS 4:13 | I can do everything through Christ, who gives me strength.

- 1 CORINTHIANS 2:9 | That is what the Scriptures mean when they say, "No eye has seen, no ear has heard, and no mind has imagined what God has prepared for those who love him."

When you're told that something will be impossible for your child . . .

- ZECHARIAH 8:6 | This is what the LORD of Heaven's Armies says: All this may seem impossible to you now. . . . But is it impossible for me?

- MATTHEW 19:26 | Jesus looked at them intently and said, "Humanly speaking, it is impossible. But with God everything is possible."

- HEBREWS 6:18 | God has given both his promise and his oath. These two things are unchangeable because it is impossible for God to lie. Therefore, we who have fled to him for refuge can have great confidence as we hold to the hope that lies before us.

The Bible is filled with seemingly impossible stories: A flood covers the earth; a sea is divided so people can walk through on dry land; the sun keeps shining until a battle can be won; a man survives three days in the belly of a fish; a virgin gives birth to a baby boy. To the person who does not believe in God or his Word, these stories defy logic. But those who believe in the Creator of all things also believe that he can alter what he has created; he can break into natural law and cause something supernatural. In order for you to recognize and experience the impossible, you need faith. Faith opens up a new dimension and allows you to understand that there's more to this world than just what you see. Suddenly, you can recognize the "impossible" things God does for his people because you believe that anything is possible for him. Learn to recognize and appreciate the "impossible" things God does for you and around you each day: unexpected forgiveness, healing for the body and heart, a moment of joy or tenderness with your child, the birth of a baby. The more you see the "impossible" acts of God with eyes of faith, the stronger your faith in him will become.

INSECURITY

When you feel like you just don't measure up to everyone else . . .

- PSALM 91:1-2 | Those who live in the shelter of the Most High will find rest in the shadow of the Almighty. This I declare about the LORD: He alone is my refuge, my place of safety; he is my God, and I trust him.

- PSALM 125:1 | Those who trust in the LORD are as secure as Mount Zion; they will not be defeated but will endure forever.

- ISAIAH 43:1-4 | Listen to the LORD who created you. . . . The one who formed you says, "Do not be afraid, for I have ransomed you. I have called you by name; you are mine. When you go through deep waters, I will be with you. When you go through rivers of difficulty, you will not drown. When you walk through the fire of oppression, you will not be burned up; the flames will not consume you. For I am the LORD, your God, the Holy One of Israel, your Savior. . . . You are precious to me. You are honored, and I love you."

When you doubt your ability to parent well . . .

- EPHESIANS 3:16-20 | I pray that from his glorious, unlimited resources he will empower you with inner strength through his Spirit. Then Christ will make his home in your hearts as you trust in him. Your roots will grow down into God's love and keep you strong. And may you have the power to understand, as all God's people should, how wide, how long, how high, and how deep his love is. May you experience the love of Christ, though it is too great to understand fully. Then you will be made complete with all the fullness of life and power that comes from God. Now all glory to God, who is able, through his mighty power at work within us, to accomplish infinitely more than we might ask or think.

When it feels as though your family will never measure up to what you see in other families . . .

- PSALM 32:8 | The LORD says, "I will guide you along the best pathway for your life. I will advise you and watch over you."

When crisis rocks your foundation and you're afraid for the future . . .

- PHILIPPIANS 4:6-7 | Don't worry about anything; instead, pray about everything. Tell God what you need, and thank him for all he has done. Then you will experience God's peace, which exceeds anything we can understand. His peace will guard your hearts and minds as you live in Christ Jesus.

When you want to help your child embrace who he or she is . . .

- EPHESIANS 2:10 | For we are God's masterpiece. He has created us anew in Christ Jesus, so we can do the good things he planned for us long ago.

- PHILIPPIANS 1:6 | I am certain that God, who began the good work within you, will continue his work until it is finally finished on the day when Christ Jesus returns.

- PSALM 37:23-24 | The LORD directs the steps of the godly. He delights in every detail of their lives. Though they stumble, they will never fall, for the LORD holds them by the hand.

- PSALM 18:19 | He led me to a place of safety; he rescued me because he delights in me.

- GENESIS 1:27 | God created human beings in his own image. In the image of God he created them; male and female he created them.

There are two aspects of the term *insecurity* in our contemporary usage. The first is insecurity in the face of life's dangers and threats; the second is insecurity concerning our worth and value. Both of these insecurities are addressed by the promises of God. You can find true security by trusting in

God's promises in the Bible because they have always proven to be true. And you and your children can find security in your worth and value because God made you in his image, gave you spiritual gifts, and promised to do his good work in you throughout your lifetime if you trust him.

INTIMACY

When you long to connect with your child in a deeper way but don't know how . . .

- PSALM 27:8 | My heart has heard you say, "Come and talk with me." And my heart responds, "LORD, I am coming."

- PSALM 147:3 | He heals the brokenhearted and bandages their wounds.

- DEUTERONOMY 33:27 | The eternal God is your refuge, and his everlasting arms are under you.

- EPHESIANS 3:19 | May you experience the love of Christ, though it is too great to understand fully. Then you will be made complete with all the fullness of life and power that comes from God.

When stress and busyness make intimacy with your spouse difficult . . .

- EPHESIANS 5:31 | The Scriptures say, "A man leaves his father and mother and is joined to his wife, and the two are united into one."

- 1 CORINTHIANS 13:4-5 | Love is patient and kind. Love is not jealous or boastful or proud or rude. It does not demand its own way. It is not irritable, and it keeps no record of being wronged.

- PROVERBS 5:15, 19 | Drink water from your own well—share your love only with your wife. . . . May you always be captivated by her love.

- GALATIANS 6:9 | Let's not get tired of doing what is good. At just the right time we will reap a harvest of blessing if we don't give up.

Time and again the Bible teaches that human beings are most fully satisfied as they experience God's unfailing love. Our deepest contentment and joy come not from the pursuit of happiness, pleasure, or material possessions, but from the pursuit of intimacy with God and others. Intimacy with God means experiencing his love to the fullest and returning that love to him. As you do this, intimacy in all your other relationships takes on new and greater meaning.

JEALOUSY

When you feel envious of families with "typical" children . . .

- PSALM 119:35 | Make me walk along the path of your commands, for that is where my happiness is found.

- PROVERBS 14:30 | A peaceful heart leads to a healthy body; jealousy is like cancer in the bones.

When contentment seems elusive . . .

- 2 CORINTHIANS 12:9-10 | Each time he said, "My grace is all you need. My power works best in weakness." So now I am glad to boast about my weaknesses, so that the power of Christ can work through me. That's why I take pleasure in my weaknesses, and in the insults, hardships, persecutions, and troubles that I suffer for Christ. For when I am weak, then I am strong.

- PSALM 1:2-3 | They delight in the law of the LORD, meditating on it day and night. They are like trees planted along the riverbank, bearing fruit each season.

When it seems there are never resources left over for you . . .

- MATTHEW 5:3 | God blesses those who are poor and realize their need for him, for the Kingdom of Heaven is theirs.

- 1 TIMOTHY 6:18-19 | Tell them to use their money to do good. They should be rich in good works and generous to those in need, always being ready to share with others. By doing this they will be storing up their treasure as a good foundation for the future so that they may experience true life.

- PSALM 23:1 | The LORD is my shepherd; I have all that I need.

You may feel jealous as you look at typical families because their circumstances may seem easier than yours. Any time you compare your situation to theirs, it gives ample opportunity for jealousy to creep into your heart. Remember that in spite of our different situations, we all need God. He wants you to recognize how much you need him because he knows that being dependent on him is a blessed way to live. Your weakness allows him to work more powerfully through you. Ask God to help you see the ways in which your life is blessed because you've been able to experience his power working through your weakness. As your focus shifts to God and what he's done for you, you will find yourself feeling more content with your own circumstances.

JOY

When you're searching for joy . . .

- PSALM 119:143 | As pressure and stress bear down on me, I find joy in your commands.

- JOHN 16:24 | You haven't done this before. Ask, using my name, and you will receive, and you will have abundant joy.

- JOHN 15:10-11 | When you obey my commandments, you remain in my love, just as I obey my Father's commandments and remain in his love. I have told you these things so that you will be filled with my joy. Yes, your joy will overflow!

- ROMANS 5:1-2 | Therefore, since we have been made right in God's sight by faith, we have peace with God because of what Jesus Christ our Lord has done for us. Because of our faith, Christ has brought us into this place of undeserved privilege where we now stand, and we confidently and joyfully look forward to sharing God's glory.

- GALATIANS 5:22 | The Holy Spirit produces this kind of fruit in our lives: love, joy . . .

When you wish someone would take joy in you . . .

- ZEPHANIAH 3:17 | The LORD your God is living among you. He is a mighty savior. He will take delight in you with gladness. With his love, he will calm all your fears. He will rejoice over you with joyful songs.

When you fear you will never smile again . . .

- JOHN 16:22 | You have sorrow now, but I will see you again; then you will rejoice, and no one can rob you of that joy.

- 1 PETER 1:6-7 | Be truly glad. There is wonderful joy ahead, even though you must endure many trials for a little while. These trials will show that your faith is genuine. It is being tested as fire tests and purifies gold—though your faith is far more precious than mere gold. So when your faith remains strong through many trials, it will bring you much praise and glory and honor on the day when Jesus Christ is revealed to the whole world.

When your cup overflows . . .

- ISAIAH 52:9 | Let the ruins of Jerusalem break into joyful song, for the LORD has comforted his people.

- PSALM 16:8-9, 11 | I know the LORD is always with me. I will not be shaken, for he is right beside me. No wonder my heart is glad, and I rejoice. . . . You will show me the way of life, granting me the joy of your presence and the pleasures of living with you forever.

God created you to have feelings, so don't be surprised when you experience emotional highs and lows. However, lasting joy and contentment run much deeper than momentary emotions. Lasting joy is like a strong current that runs deep beneath the stormy surface of your feelings. It is sharing with others the blessings of God's presence. Joy is the sense of security that comes only from being held by an almighty God. It is the peace of knowing that God accepts you and wants you to be with him forever. It is the quiet confidence you experience when you let God guide you at all times and in all things, trusting that his direction is in the best interests of you and your child. No emotional ups and downs can shake that kind of strong foundation.

JUDGMENT

When others criticize you or your child . . .

- LUKE 6:37 | Do not judge others, and you will not be judged. Do not condemn others, or it will all come back against you. Forgive others, and you will be forgiven.

- COLOSSIANS 3:13 | Make allowance for each other's faults, and forgive anyone who offends you. Remember, the Lord forgave you, so you must forgive others.

- PSALM 139:17 | How precious are your thoughts about me, O God. They cannot be numbered!

When people blame your child's behavior on bad parenting . . .

- ROMANS 8:33-34 | Who dares accuse us whom God has chosen for his own? No one—for God himself has given us right standing with himself. Who then will condemn us? No one—for Christ Jesus died for us and was raised to life for us, and he is sitting in the place of honor at God's right hand, pleading for us.

- JOHN 9:2-3 | "Rabbi," his disciples asked him, "why was this man born blind? Was it because of his own sins or his parents' sins?" "It was not because of his sins or his parents' sins," Jesus answered. "This happened so the power of God could be seen in him."

When you're tempted to judge others who complain about problems that seem trite . . .

- MATTHEW 7:1-2 | Do not judge others, and you will not be judged. For you will be treated as you treat others. The standard you use in judging is the standard by which you will be judged.

- 1 CORINTHIANS 4:5 | Don't make judgments about anyone ahead of time—before the Lord returns. For he will bring our darkest secrets to light and will reveal our private motives. Then God will give to each one whatever praise is due.

When you're tempted to judge your child by what you see . . .

- 1 SAMUEL 16:7 | The LORD doesn't see things the way you see them. People judge by outward appearance, but the LORD looks at the heart.

When we cast judgment, we often jump to conclusions without knowing the full story. Perhaps you are wrestling with judging others for complaining about small issues when they know your life is filled with significant challenges. God says that the standard by which you judge others is the standard by which he judges you. God looks at the heart. If you've been on the receiving end of someone's wrongful criticism, you know how painful it can be. The only way to end the cycle is through forgiveness and awareness. You can be less shaken by judgment because you know God sees your heart. Get to know someone's story, and be willing to share your own. The more people understand, the less likely they are to judge.

KNOWING GOD

When you wonder if your child will have a relationship with God . . .

- 1 CORINTHIANS 12:6 | God works in different ways, but it is the same God who does the work in all of us.

- LUKE 19:10 | The Son of Man came to seek and save those who are lost.

- ROMANS 8:39 | No power in the sky above or in the earth below—indeed, nothing in all creation will ever be able to separate us from the love of God that is revealed in Christ Jesus our Lord.

When you're ready to go deeper with God . . .

- ROMANS 10:9-10 | If you openly declare that Jesus is Lord and believe in your heart that God raised him from the dead, you will be saved. For it is by believing in your heart that you are made right with God, and it is by openly declaring your faith that you are saved.

- 1 CORINTHIANS 2:10-12 | It was to us that God revealed these things by his Spirit. For his Spirit searches out everything and shows us God's deep secrets. No one can know a person's thoughts except that person's own spirit, and no one can know God's thoughts except God's own

Spirit. And we have received God's Spirit (not the world's spirit), so we can know the wonderful things God has freely given us.

- EPHESIANS 3:17-19 | Then Christ will make his home in your hearts as you trust in him. Your roots will grow down into God's love and keep you strong. And may you have the power to understand, as all God's people should, how wide, how long, how high, and how deep his love is. May you experience the love of Christ, though it is too great to understand fully. Then you will be made complete with all the fullness of life and power that comes from God.

God is all about relationship. He is not an elusive being; he is a God who desires to be known. His love is personal, and he wants all of his children to experience his personal touch in their lives. In God's wisdom, he knows how to connect with each person he's created, even if they have trouble communicating verbally or connecting emotionally. Trust that he is deeply in love with your child. If you're hungering for a deeper connection with God, he is ready to share his heart with you, lead you by his Spirit, and help you understand more about who he is and his plans for your life. Open your heart to him and trust him.

LETTING GO

If special needs parenting isn't the path you dreamed of . . .

- ISAIAH 43:18-19 | Forget all that—it is nothing compared to what I am going to do. For I am about to do something new. See, I have already begun! Do you not see it? I will make a pathway through the wilderness. I will create rivers in the dry wasteland.

When obedience to God's direction requires you to let go of old habits . . .

- HEBREWS 12:1-2 | Therefore, since we are surrounded by such a huge crowd of witnesses to the life of faith, let us strip off every weight that slows us down, especially the sin that so easily trips us up. And let us run with endurance the race God has set before us. We do this by keeping our eyes on Jesus, the champion who initiates and perfects our faith.

- PROVERBS 16:3 | Commit your actions to the LORD, and your plans will succeed.

Letting go is a difficult and painful process. It feels risky to give up a comfortable habit or a long-desired dream in your heart. You may wonder who you are without those things. Sometimes you need to let go of your old ways so you can receive a new way from God. It may look scary at first. Give your broken dreams to God, and let him lead you to a new dream for you and your family. Surrender the patterns of your life to God, and give him the authority to form new patterns designed to strengthen and perfect your faith. If God can make a pathway through the wilderness, if he can part the seas, he is able to refresh you and give you new life.

LIMITATIONS
When your child's disability seems so meaningless . . .

- JOHN 11:4 | When Jesus heard about it he said, "Lazarus's sickness will not end in death. No, it happened for the glory of God so that the Son of God will receive glory from this."

- 1 CORINTHIANS 15:58 | So, my dear brothers and sisters, be strong and immovable. Always work enthusiastically for the Lord, for you know that nothing you do for the Lord is ever useless.

- JEREMIAH 1:5 | I knew you before I formed you in your mother's womb. Before you were born I set you apart and appointed you . . .

- REVELATION 21:5 | The one sitting on the throne said, "Look, I am making everything new!"

When your strength runs out . . .

- ISAIAH 40:28-29 | Have you never heard? Have you never understood? The LORD is the everlasting God, the Creator of all the earth. He never grows weak or weary. No one can measure the depths of his understanding. He gives power to the weak and strength to the powerless.

When it feels like there's a limit to what God can do . . .

- ROMANS 11:36 | Everything comes from him and exists by his power and is intended for his glory.

- 2 CORINTHIANS 4:7 | We now have this light shining in our hearts, but we ourselves are like fragile clay jars containing this great treasure. This makes it clear that our great power is from God, not from ourselves.

When you need godly parameters for your life . . .

- EPHESIANS 4:31-32 | Get rid of all bitterness, rage, anger, harsh words, and slander, as well as all types of evil behavior. Instead, be kind to each other, tenderhearted, forgiving one another, just as God through Christ has forgiven you.

As a parent of a child with special needs, the word *limitations* may mean so many things to you. You may fight this word in your home or school as you try to help your child embrace and live above his limitations. You may talk about the limits of your energy, finances, resources, and support. But in God's mind, your limitations are opportunities for his unlimited power and grace to shine through you. You have the power and presence of the unlimited Creator of the world living in you. The cracks in your strength allow that power to shine through and bring God glory as he helps you and your child overcome your limitations.

LONELINESS
When it seems like no one is on your side . . .

- PSALM 27:10 | Even if my father and mother abandon me, the LORD will hold me close.

- JUDGES 6:16 | I will be with you.

- PSALM 16:8 | I know the LORD is always with me. I will not be shaken, for he is right beside me.

When you feel forgotten . . .

- ISAIAH 49:15-16 | Can a mother forget her nursing child? Can she feel no love for the child she has borne? But even if that were possible, I would not forget you! See, I have written your name on the palms of my hands.

When you or your child has been rejected . . .

- JEREMIAH 30:17, 22 | "I will give you back your health and heal your wounds," says the LORD. "For you are called an outcast . . . [but] you will be my people, and I will be your God."

- LUKE 6:22-23 | What blessings await you when people hate you and exclude you and mock you and curse you as evil because you follow the Son of Man. When that happens, be happy! Yes, leap for joy! For a great reward awaits you in heaven. And remember, their ancestors treated the ancient prophets that same way.

- DEUTERONOMY 31:8 | Do not be afraid or discouraged, for the LORD will personally go ahead of you. He will be with you; he will neither fail you nor abandon you.

When you need a friend . . .

- JAMES 4:8 | Come close to God, and God will come close to you.

Being a parent of a child with special needs can be lonely at times. You may feel you are the only one fighting for your child's needs. You may sense that your friends have backed away because they don't know how to help or what to say. You may experience the discouragement of your child being rejected by peers because he or she is different. When you are lonely and in need of friendship, you can always draw close to God because he promises never to leave your side. When family and friends back away, God pursues you and moves closer. Lean into him and remember you are not forgotten, you are not abandoned, and you are not alone.

LOSS
When it feels as if you've lost everything . . .

- HEBREWS 10:34-36 | You suffered along with those who were thrown into jail, and when all you owned was taken from you, you accepted it with joy. You knew there were better things waiting for you that will last forever. So do not throw away this confident trust in the Lord. Remember the great reward it brings you! Patient endurance is what you need now, so that you will continue to do God's will. Then you will receive all that he has promised.

- Psalm 27:4-5 | The one thing I ask of the Lord—the thing I seek most—is to live in the house of the Lord all the days of my life. . . . For he will conceal me there when troubles come.

When you live in fear of what you can lose . . .

- Mark 8:34-36 | Then, calling the crowd to join his disciples, he said, "If any of you wants to be my follower, you must give up your own way, take up your cross, and follow me. If you try to hang on to your life, you will lose it. But if you give up your life for my sake and for the sake of the Good News, you will save it. And what do you benefit if you gain the whole world but lose your own soul?"

When you wonder where to turn in the emptiness . . .

- Jeremiah 39:18 | Because you trusted me, I will give you your life as a reward. I will rescue you and keep you safe. I, the Lord, have spoken!

- Philippians 2:13 | God is working in you, giving you the desire and the power to do what pleases him.

- John 10:10 | The thief's purpose is to steal and kill and destroy. My purpose is to give them a rich and satisfying life.

When your child regresses and loses skills . . .

- PSALM 39:7 | Lord, where do I put my hope? My only hope is in you.

- JOHN 16:33 | I have told you all this so that you may have peace in me. Here on earth you will have many trials and sorrows. But take heart, because I have overcome the world.

- ROMANS 5:3-5 | We can rejoice, too, when we run into problems and trials, for we know that they help us develop endurance. And endurance develops strength of character, and character strengthens our confident hope of salvation. And this hope will not lead to disappointment. For we know how dearly God loves us, because he has given us the Holy Spirit to fill our hearts with his love.

In times of great loss, you may be tempted to give up on God. You may doubt him and wonder why he didn't prevent this loss. The Bible tells you that troubles will come—things will be lost and your feelings will be hurt. Yet the Bible also encourages you not to throw out your confident hope. When you are grieving and fear the emptiness ahead, seek refuge in the presence of God. He is a God who rewards those who trust when it hurts and cling to him when they have nothing else. You have this hope: God loves to redeem great loss for abundant blessing.

LOVE

When you worry that your love for your child isn't enough . . .

- 1 JOHN 4:17 | As we live in God, our love grows more perfect. So we will not be afraid on the day of judgment, but we can face him with confidence because we live like Jesus here in this world.

When you feel unlovable . . .

- JOHN 3:16 | This is how God loved the world: He gave his one and only Son, so that everyone who believes in him will not perish but have eternal life.

- ROMANS 8:38-39 | I am convinced that nothing can ever separate us from God's love. Neither death nor life, neither angels nor demons, neither our fears for today nor our worries about tomorrow—not even the powers of hell can separate us from God's love. No power in the sky above or in the earth below—indeed, nothing in all creation will ever be able to separate us from the love of God that is revealed in Christ Jesus our Lord.

When you wonder what real love looks like . . .

- 1 JOHN 4:9-10 | God showed how much he loved us by sending his one and only Son into the world so that we might have eternal life through him. This is real love—not that we loved God, but that he loved us and sent his Son as a sacrifice to take away our sins.

- 1 CORINTHIANS 13:4-7 | Love is patient and kind. Love is not jealous or boastful or proud or rude. It does not demand its own way. It is not irritable, and it keeps no record of being wronged. It does not rejoice about injustice but rejoices whenever the truth wins out. Love never gives up, never loses faith, is always hopeful, and endures through every circumstance.

- EPHESIANS 5:1-2 | Imitate God, therefore, in everything you do, because you are his dear children. Live a life filled with love, following the example of Christ. He loved us and offered himself as a sacrifice for us, a pleasing aroma to God.

When someone in your life is hard to love . . .

- LUKE 6:32, 35 | If you love only those who love you, why should you get credit for that? Even sinners love those who love them! . . . Love your enemies! Do good to them. Lend to them without expecting to be repaid. Then your reward from heaven will be very great, and you will truly be acting as children of the Most High, for he is kind to those who are unthankful and wicked.

Love can feel complicated when you're dealing with special needs. You may feel your love for your child just isn't enough. You may feel your love falter when your child displays difficult behavioral issues. Or your child may make you feel just plain unlovable. If you're struggling to love and be loved, you first need the truth of the gospel to sink deep into your soul: You are loved. This changes everything. Nothing can separate you from God's love. Jesus loved you so much that he gave up his life to save yours, and he lovingly pursued you before you ever acknowledged him. God also delights in taking the love you offer and blessing and growing it. He enables you to live a life that is full of love. Only by letting God's love flow through you and asking him for more of it will you be able to love beyond what you are capable of on your own.

MARRIAGE

When you are thankful for your spouse . . .

- GENESIS 2:24 | This explains why a man leaves his father and mother and is joined to his wife, and the two are united into one.

- 1 CORINTHIANS 13:7 | Love never gives up, never loses faith, is always hopeful, and endures through every circumstance.

When your child's needs leave no room for you to meet your spouse's needs . . .

- PHILIPPIANS 2:13 | God is working in you, giving you the desire and the power to do what pleases him.

- COLOSSIANS 1:11 | We also pray that you will be strengthened with all his glorious power so you will have all the endurance and patience you need.

- EPHESIANS 4:2 | Always be humble and gentle. Be patient with each other, making allowance for each other's faults because of your love.

When you want to strengthen your marriage . . .

- 1 PETER 4:8 | Most important of all, continue to show deep love for each other, for love covers a multitude of sins.

- COLOSSIANS 3:14 | Above all, clothe yourselves with love, which binds us all together in perfect harmony.

When the stresses of your marriage make you wonder if being married to someone else would be better . . .

- HEBREWS 13:4 | Give honor to marriage, and remain faithful to one another in marriage. God will surely judge people who are immoral and those who commit adultery.

- 2 THESSALONIANS 3:3 | The Lord is faithful; he will strengthen you and guard you from the evil one.

When marriage feels lonely . . .

- ISAIAH 54:5-6 | "For your Creator will be your husband; the LORD of Heaven's Armies is his name! He is your Redeemer, the Holy One of Israel, the God of all the earth. For the LORD has called you back from your grief—as though you were a young wife abandoned by her husband," says your God.

- ISAIAH 54:10 | "For the mountains may move and the hills disappear, but even then my faithful love for you will remain. My covenant of blessing will never be broken," says the LORD, who has mercy on you.

The strength of your marriage is essential to the health of your family. When your child's needs are so urgent, it can be easy to put your marriage on the back burner. While this may be necessary for a season, it can lead to feelings of loneliness or even temptation to wander away from your spouse. If your marriage seems lifeless, start by asking God to breathe new life into your relationship. A godly marriage pleases the Lord, and he loves supplying his people with the power and desire to do what pleases him. Find ways to build marriage habits based on respect for God and his Word and to respond to each other with love and kindness. God is faithful, and his desire is for your marriage to thrive and leave a legacy that extends to future generations.

MERCY

When your child's behavior makes it hard to show mercy . . .

- MATTHEW 5:7 | God blesses those who are merciful, for they will be shown mercy.

When you can't forgive yourself and doubt God will either . . .

- PSALM 103:8-10 | The LORD is compassionate and merciful, slow to get angry and filled with unfailing love. He will not constantly accuse us, nor remain angry forever. He does not punish us for all our sins; he does not deal harshly with us, as we deserve.

When you need to be refreshed by the undeserved kindness of God . . .

- PSALM 119:132 | Come and show me your mercy, as you do for all who love your name.

- MICAH 7:18 | Where is another God like you, who pardons . . . guilt . . . overlooking the sins of his . . . people? You will not stay angry with your people forever, because you delight in showing unfailing love.

- PSALM 103:12-13 | He has removed our sins as far from us as the east is from the west. The LORD is like a father to his children, tender and compassionate to those who fear him.

Mercy is relentless kindness. It has no regard for achievements or failures—it is kind just the same. It offers forgiveness and grace even when you do not deserve them. God is so merciful. When you mess up, he doesn't point fingers or keep score of your shortcomings. He is patient with you and loves you despite them. Nothing you do will put you out of the reach of God's forgiveness if you will only ask for it. And when you experience God's mercy, you can extend it to others, too. Does your child need a merciful response from you? Showing mercy opens doors for God to bless you as well.

MOTIVES

When what drives you to keep going as a special needs parent isn't for the right reasons . . .

- 2 THESSALONIANS 1:11-12 | We keep on praying for you, asking our God to enable you to live a life worthy of his call. May he give you the power to accomplish all the good things your faith prompts you to do. Then the name of our Lord Jesus will be honored because of the way you live, and you will be honored along with him.

This is all made possible because of the grace of our God and Lord, Jesus Christ.

When you help because you're tired of being the one needing help . . .

- PSALM 86:11 | Teach me your ways, O LORD, that I may live according to your truth! Grant me purity of heart, so that I may honor you.

When you wonder what motives honor God . . .

- JEREMIAH 17:10 | I, the LORD, search all hearts and examine secret motives. I give all people their due rewards, according to what their actions deserve.

- 1 CHRONICLES 29:17 | I know, my God, that you examine our hearts and rejoice when you find integrity there.

- MATTHEW 22:37-39 | Jesus replied, "'You must love the LORD your God with all your heart, all your soul, and all your mind.' This is the first and greatest commandment. A second is equally important: 'Love your neighbor as yourself.'"

The worthiest motive of all is to honor God. Sometimes we are driven by fear, praise, recognition, bragging rights, or just some relief! Maybe you react a certain way to your child because you want others to think you're a good parent, or you help out at school because you want the teacher to like you. When what drives you is based more on people's approval than on God's, you know your motives are influenced by unworthy goals. If this sounds like you, begin asking God to search your heart and show you where you are motivated by less worthy goals. Ask him to give you fresh motivation to live for him and to quiet the voices that divert your motivations away from him.

NEEDS
When your family needs more than you can give . . .

- PSALM 138:3 | As soon as I pray, you answer me; you encourage me by giving me strength.

- PHILIPPIANS 4:19 | This same God who takes care of me will supply all your needs from his glorious riches, which have been given to us in Christ Jesus.

When your personal needs are unmet . . .

- 2 CORINTHIANS 9:8 | God will generously provide all you need. Then you will always have everything you need and plenty left over to share with others.

When your needs are urgent . . .

- ISAIAH 65:24 | I will answer them before they even call to me. While they are still talking about their needs, I will go ahead and answer their prayers!

- PSALM 40:17 | As for me, since I am poor and needy, let the Lord keep me in his thoughts. You are my helper and my savior. O my God, do not delay.

When you focus more on your problems than your Provider . . .

- PSALM 23:1 | The LORD is my shepherd; I have all that I need.

- MATTHEW 6:33 | Seek the Kingdom of God above all else, and live righteously, and he will give you everything you need.

When you feel like you have to fight dirty to get your child what he or she needs. . .

- 1 JOHN 5:3-5 | Loving God means keeping his commandments, and his commandments are not burdensome. For every child of God defeats this evil world, and we achieve this victory through our faith. And who can win this battle against the world? Only those who believe that Jesus is the Son of God.

When you wonder how God feels about the needy . . .

- PSALM 72:12-14 | He will rescue the poor when they cry to him; he will help the oppressed, who have no one to defend them. He feels pity for the weak and the needy, and he will rescue them. He will redeem them from oppression and violence, for their lives are precious to him.

When you feel you need a new life . . .

- TITUS 3:4-7 | When God our Savior revealed his kindness and love, he saved us, not because of the righteous things we had done, but because of his mercy. He washed away our sins, giving us a new birth and new life through the Holy Spirit. He generously poured out the Spirit upon us through Jesus Christ our Savior. Because of his grace he made us right in his sight and gave us confidence that we will inherit eternal life.

You are precious to God. He cares about the things you and your child need. God is generous, and you can be sure he is compassionate toward the needy. Your needs are opportunities to experience God's provision from his glorious riches and from his body, the church. What a blessing to see with your own eyes the help of your Savior when he meets those needs in your life. When the needs of your family are overwhelming, tell God all about it. Even though he already knows, it is often through your conversation with him that he settles your soul and helps you wait for his rescue. You can be confident he will not abandon you in your time of need.

NORMAL

When worry and stress become your new normal . . .

- LUKE 12:25-28 | Can all your worries add a single moment to your life? And if worry can't accomplish a little thing like that, what's the use of worrying over bigger things? Look at the lilies and how they grow. They don't work or make their clothing, yet Solomon in all his glory was not dressed as beautifully as they are. And if God cares so wonderfully for flowers that are here today and thrown into the fire tomorrow, he will certainly care for you.

When you grow restless in your usual routine . . .

- PSALM 145:13-14 | The LORD always keeps his promises; he is gracious in all he does. The LORD helps the fallen and lifts those bent beneath their loads.

- PSALM 40:1-2 | I waited patiently for the LORD to help me, and he turned to me and heard my cry. He lifted me out of the pit of despair, out of the mud and the mire. He set my feet on solid ground and steadied me as I walked along.

When you wish your family could be more typical . . .

- ISAIAH 43:1 | The one who formed you says, "Do not be afraid, for I have ransomed you. I have called you by name; you are mine."

- PHILIPPIANS 3:20-21 | We are citizens of heaven, where the Lord Jesus Christ lives. And we are eagerly waiting for him to return as our Savior. He will take our weak mortal bodies and change them into glorious bodies like his own, using the same power with which he will bring everything under his control.

- 1 CORINTHIANS 12:1, 4, 6-7, 11, 18, 22, 27 | Now, dear brothers and sisters, regarding . . . the special abilities the Spirit gives us. . . . There are different kinds of spiritual gifts. . . . God works in different ways, but it is the same God who does the work in all of us. A spiritual gift is given to each of us so we can help each other. . . . It is the one and only Spirit who distributes all these gifts. He alone decides which gift each person should have. . . . Our bodies have many parts, and God has put each part just where he wants it. . . . In fact, some of the parts of the body that seem weakest and least important are actually the most necessary. . . . All of you together are Christ's body, and each of you is a part of it.

When others judge you or your child for being different . . .

- PSALM 139:13-14, 17 | You made all the delicate, inner parts of my body and knit me together in my mother's womb. Thank you for making me so wonderfully complex! Your workmanship is marvelous—how well I know it. . . . How precious are your thoughts about me, O God. They cannot be numbered!

Blending in with everyone else was never God's intention for those who believe in him. This world is obsessed with keeping up with what's normal. Yet throughout the Bible, God asks his people to be different, to be set apart, to be special. Being a special needs parent isn't a typical parenting journey by any means. Perhaps, though, it is a blessing to never have to wrestle with the illusion of normalcy. You are keenly aware of how your family is special. It can be a tough road to walk; the rhythms and routines of caregiving can create a stressful and exhausting norm. Your God, who calls you to be set apart for him, also provides the strength and patience to walk a different road than those around you. You are precious to God, and he has knit you and your child together in ways that bring him glory. Your goal in this life isn't to fit in and look like everyone else. You were made to stand out for God's glory.

OBEDIENCE

When you know what's right but don't want to do it . . .

- JAMES 1:22-25 | Don't just listen to God's word. You must do what it says. Otherwise, you are only fooling yourselves. For if you listen to the word and don't obey, it is like glancing at your face in a mirror. You see yourself, walk away, and forget what you look like. But if you look carefully into the perfect law that sets you free, and if you do what it says and don't forget what you heard, then God will bless you for doing it.

When submitting to God means suffering . . .

- DEUTERONOMY 7:9 | Understand, therefore, that the LORD your God is indeed God. He is the faithful God who keeps his covenant for a thousand generations and lavishes his unfailing love on those who love him and obey his commands.

- HEBREWS 5:8 | Even though Jesus was God's Son, he learned obedience from the things he suffered.

- 1 PETER 3:14 | Even if you suffer for doing what is right, God will reward you for it. So don't worry or be afraid.

When you become a slave to your family's needs rather than a servant of God . . .

- EZEKIEL 36:25-27 | Then I will sprinkle clean water on you, and you will be clean. Your filth will be washed away, and you will no longer worship idols. And I will give you a new heart, and I will put a new spirit in you. I will take out your stony, stubborn heart and give you a tender, responsive heart. And I will put my Spirit in you so that you will follow my decrees and be careful to obey my regulations.

When you're tempted to sin because you feel you deserve a little happiness . . .

- PSALM 119:2 | Joyful are those who obey his laws and search for him with all their hearts.

- PSALM 119:35 | Make me walk along the path of your commands, for that is where my happiness is found.

When your willpower to obey God is weak . . .

- JOB 17:9 | The righteous keep moving forward, and those with clean hands become stronger and stronger.

God's ways are not meant to be burdensome. He lovingly gives you boundaries just as parents protect and guide their children to keep them safe. God desires obedience motivated by love and trust, not by fear. Ironically, obedience actually frees us to enjoy life as God intended because it keeps us from becoming enslaved to harmful situations that cause heartache. It's tempting to think that happiness is found in the freedom to do what you want. But God's ways point out the path to joyful and peaceful living. When you know what God requires and you make obedience a practice, it becomes a blessed way of living.

OVERCOMING

When the obstacles to healing seem insurmountable . . .

- JEREMIAH 32:27 | I am the LORD, the God of all the peoples of the world. Is anything too hard for me?

- PSALM 116:3-5 | Death wrapped its ropes around me; the terrors of the grave overtook me. I saw only trouble and sorrow. Then I called on the name of the LORD: "Please, LORD, save me!" How kind the LORD is! How good he is! So merciful, this God of ours!

When old habits are hard to overcome . . .

- PSALM 51:1, 10 | Have mercy on me, O God, because of your unfailing love. Because of your great compassion, blot out the stain of my sins. . . . Create in me a clean heart, O God. Renew a loyal spirit within me.

- JEREMIAH 3:22 | "My wayward children," says the LORD, "come back to me, and I will heal your wayward hearts."

When you're up against a huge challenge in your child's life . . .

- 1 CHRONICLES 28:20 | Be strong and courageous, and do the work. Don't be afraid or discouraged, for the LORD God, my God, is with you. He will not fail you or forsake you.

When your battle plan begins to unravel . . .

- PSALM 46:1-2 | God is our refuge and strength, always ready to help in times of trouble. So we will not fear when earthquakes come and the mountains crumble into the sea.

As a parent of a child with special needs, you want your child to overcome obstacles to his or her development. You probably fight for this daily. When you're up against big challenges, remember that God is with you; he is your safe place and your source of strength. The key to overcoming battles is living a life surrendered to God. When you begin to see the obstacles as opportunities for God to show his power, they will not seem so overwhelming. The very hardships and weaknesses that frighten you may be the tools God wants to use.

PAIN

When the pain seems pointless . . .

- 2 CORINTHIANS 1:4-6 | He comforts us in all our troubles so that we can comfort others. When they are troubled, we will be able to give them the same comfort God has given us. For the more we suffer for Christ, the more God will shower us with his comfort through Christ. Even when we are weighed down with troubles, it is for your comfort and salvation!

When your child is in physical pain . . .

- PSALM 10:17 | LORD, you know the hopes of the helpless. Surely you will hear their cries and comfort them.

- PSALM 69:29 | I am suffering and in pain. Rescue me, O God, by your saving power.

When you endure the emotional pain of a child with mental health issues . . .

- PSALM 107:10, 14-15 | Some sat in darkness and deepest gloom, imprisoned in iron chains of misery. . . . He led them from the darkness and deepest gloom; he snapped their chains. Let them praise the LORD for his great love and for the wonderful things he has done for them.

- PSALM 40:1-2 | I waited patiently for the LORD to help me, and he turned to me and heard my cry. He lifted me out of the pit of despair, out of the mud and the mire. He set my feet on solid ground and steadied me as I walked along.

When you experience painful daily reminders of your child's needs . . .

- PSALM 70:5 | As for me, I am poor and needy; please hurry to my aid, O God. You are my helper and my savior; O LORD, do not delay.

- PSALM 73:14, 23, 26 | I get nothing but trouble all day long; every morning brings me pain. . . . Yet I still belong to you; you hold my right hand. . . . My health may fail, and my spirit may grow weak, but God remains the strength of my heart; he is mine forever.

Pain is an inevitable part of the journey as a parent of a child with special needs. You ache when your child suffers physically, or when he or she experiences the emotional pain of sacrifice or rejection. However, God promises that you are never left alone in your pain. The hurt points to your need for God's comfort and to the promise that your suffering will end one day. Give him your burdens, hold on to him tighter, and let him take care of you through the pain you experience each day.

PATIENCE
When you're waiting for answers . . .

- LAMENTATIONS 3:25-26 | The LORD is good to those who depend on him, to those who search for him. So it is good to wait quietly for salvation from the LORD.

- ROMANS 8:23-26, 28 | We, too, wait with eager hope for the day when God will give us our full rights as his adopted children. . . . (If we already have something, we don't need to hope for it. But if we look forward to something we don't yet have, we must wait patiently and confidently.) And the Holy Spirit helps us in our weakness. . . . And we know that God causes everything to work together for the good of those who love God and are called according to his purpose for them.

- ROMANS 15:4 | The Scriptures give us hope and encouragement as we wait patiently for God's promises to be fulfilled.

When you lose your temper . . .

- ISAIAH 1:18 | Though your sins are like scarlet, I will make them as white as snow.

- MARK 3:28 | I tell you the truth, all sin . . . can be forgiven.

- PSALM 86:5 | O Lord, you are so good, so ready to forgive, so full of unfailing love for all who ask for your help.

When you don't know if you can tolerate another meltdown . . .

- 2 SAMUEL 22:7 | In my distress I cried out to the LORD; yes I cried to my God for help. He heard me from his sanctuary; my cry reached his ears.

When you wonder if all your efforts matter . . .

- JAMES 5:7-8 | Dear brothers and sisters, be patient as you wait for the Lord's return. Consider the farmers who patiently wait for the rains in the fall and in the spring. They eagerly look for the valuable harvest to ripen. You, too, must be patient. Take courage, for the coming of the Lord is near.

Patience has to be developed like a muscle—it grows stronger through practice. As a parent of a child with special needs, perhaps you feel your patience being constantly tested and pushed to the limits. Remember that God is infinitely patient with you and is always ready to forgive and support you. Rely on his strength to help you respond with patience as you wait for his best plans to unfold in your life and in the life of your child.

PEACE

When you struggle to be at peace with being a parent of a child with special needs . . .

- JOHN 14:27 | I am leaving you with a gift—peace of mind and heart. And the peace I give is a gift the world cannot give. So don't be troubled or afraid.

When the stress makes you sick . . .

- ISAIAH 58:11 | The LORD will guide you continually, giving you water when you are dry and restoring your strength. You will be like a well-watered garden, like an ever-flowing spring.

- PSALM 73:26 | My health may fail, and my spirit may grow weak, but God remains the strength of my heart; he is mine forever.

When panic strikes again . . .

- LAMENTATIONS 3:57 | Yes, you came when I called; you told me, "Do not fear."

When chaos prevents you from rest . . .

- PSALM 3:5 | I lay down and slept, yet I woke up in safety, for the LORD was watching over me.

- 2 PETER 1:2 | May God give you more and more grace and peace as you grow in your knowledge of God and Jesus our Lord.

- PSALM 16:8-9 | I know the LORD is always with me. I will not be shaken, for he is right beside me. No wonder my heart is glad, and I rejoice. My body rests in safety.

When you want peace to replace conflict in your relationships . . .

- 2 CORINTHIANS 13:11 | Be joyful. Grow to maturity. Encourage each other. Live in harmony and peace. Then the God of love and peace will be with you.

- JAMES 3:17-18 | The wisdom from above is first of
  all pure. It is also peace loving, gentle at all times,
  and willing to yield to others. It is full of mercy and
  the fruit of good deeds. It shows no favoritism and
  is always sincere. And those who are peacemakers
  will plant seeds of peace and reap a harvest of
  righteousness.

As a parent of a child with special needs, you may find
peace hard to come by. Perhaps you're dealing with worry
or your home is filled with tension. Jesus has more in mind
for you. He is the source of peace, and he promises to be
with you in crises and help you find the calmness of heart
only he can give. The world will tempt you with its defini-
tion of peace, which is to discard your responsibilities and
live only for yourself. But that doesn't lead to peace; it leads
to emptiness, guilt, and regret. Peace of mind and heart
come from inviting God—the source of peace—to live in
you and help you understand that this world is only temporary. Then you can navigate through any chaos because
you know God is ultimately in control and you are living
the way you were created to live.

PERSEVERANCE

When you need a fresh perspective to help you press on . . .

- 2 CORINTHIANS 4:16-18 | That is why we never give up. Though our bodies are dying, our spirits are being renewed every day. For our present troubles are small and won't last very long. Yet they produce for us a glory that vastly outweighs them and will last forever! So we don't look at the troubles we can see now; rather, we fix our gaze on things that cannot be seen. For the things we see now will soon be gone, but the things we cannot see will last forever.

- JAMES 1:2-4 | Dear brothers and sisters, when troubles of any kind come your way, consider it an opportunity for great joy. For you know that when your faith is tested, your endurance has a chance to grow. So let it grow, for when your endurance is fully developed, you will be perfect and complete, needing nothing.

When your caregiving doesn't seem to make a difference anymore . . .

- 1 CORINTHIANS 13:7 | Love never gives up, never loses faith, is always hopeful, and endures through every circumstance.

- GALATIANS 6:9 | Let's not get tired of doing what is good. At just the right time we will reap a harvest of blessing if we don't give up.

When you need someone to lean on today . . .

- NAHUM 1:7 | The LORD is good, a strong refuge when trouble comes. He is close to those who trust in him.

- JOHN 15:5 | Yes, I am the vine; you are the branches. Those who remain in me, and I in them, will produce much fruit. For apart from me you can do nothing.

When you keep praying for your child no matter how hopeless things seem . . .

- MATTHEW 7:7-8 | Keep on asking, and you will receive what you ask for. Keep on seeking, and you will find. Keep on knocking, and the door will be opened to you. For everyone who asks, receives. Everyone who seeks, finds. And to everyone who knocks, the door will be opened.

As a parent of a child with special needs, you may practice perseverance more than anyone! Each day brings challenges that you must move through for the sake of your child and your family. Even when it seems like your efforts make no difference, God promises to reward those who continue to do what is right and good despite a seeming lack of success.

He promises you will grow and be fruitful when you press on with him with a hopeful and trusting heart.

POWER OF GOD

When you need supernatural strength . . .

- PSALM 60:12 | With God's help we will do mighty things.

- COLOSSIANS 1:27, 29 | This is the secret: Christ lives in you. This gives you assurance of sharing his glory. . . . That's why I work and struggle so hard, depending on Christ's mighty power that works within me.

- 1 CORINTHIANS 1:24 | To those called by God to salvation, . . . Christ is the power of God and the wisdom of God.

When the world seems like a dark place . . .

- 1 JOHN 4:4 | The Spirit who lives in you is greater than the spirit who lives in the world.

- 2 CORINTHIANS 4:6 | God, who said, "Let there be light in the darkness," has made this light shine in our hearts so we could know the glory of God that is seen in the face of Jesus Christ.

When you wonder if there's a purpose behind your child's weaknesses . . .

- JOHN 9:3, 5 | "It was not because of his sins or his parents' sins," Jesus answered. "This happened so the power of God could be seen in him. . . . But while I am here in the world, I am the light of the world."

When you want to see how powerful God is . . .

- PSALM 147:4-5 | He counts the stars and calls them all by name. How great is our Lord! His power is absolute! His understanding is beyond comprehension!

- PSALM 29:10-11 | The LORD rules over the floodwaters. The LORD reigns as king forever. The LORD gives his people strength. The LORD blesses them with peace.

- ROMANS 6:8-9 | Since we died with Christ, we know we will also live with him. We are sure of this because Christ was raised from the dead, and he will never die again. Death no longer has any power over him.

No matter your child's special needs, you are not without resources. God's power—the wisdom that formed the world and the strength that raised Jesus from the dead—is available to you! You may see your weaknesses and struggles, but God's power has already overcome them all. He offers strength, wisdom, and power to those surrendered to him for the purpose of glorifying him.

PRAYER

When you wonder if God notices when you talk to him . . .

- PSALM 34:15 | The eyes of the LORD watch over those who do right; his ears are open to their cries for help.

- PSALM 116:1-2 | I love the LORD because he hears my voice and my prayer for mercy. Because he bends down to listen, I will pray as long as I have breath!

- PSALM 9:12 | He does not ignore the cries of those who suffer.

When you want your heart to be in tune with God's heart . . .

- 1 JOHN 5:14 | We are confident that he hears us whenever we ask for anything that pleases him.

- JOHN 15:7 | If you remain in me and my words remain in you, you may ask for anything you want, and it will be granted!

When you wonder if your prayers for your child make a difference . . .

- JAMES 5:16 | The earnest prayer of a righteous person has great power and produces wonderful results.

When you need a friend to talk to . . .

- PHILIPPIANS 4:6-7 | Tell God what you need, and thank him for all he has done. Then you will experience God's peace, which exceeds anything we can understand. His peace will guard your hearts and minds as you live in Christ Jesus.

In times of prayer, you are connecting relationally to God. When you talk with God, you are tuned in to who he is and how he sees you and those you pray for. Your posture bends the knee to God's will, your desires are shaped to reflect his will, and you receive peace knowing God is truly listening. Your prayers are not in vain!

PRESENCE OF GOD

When you face problems that are bigger than you can handle alone . . .

- DEUTERONOMY 7:21 | Do not be afraid . . . for the LORD your God is among you, and he is a great and awesome God.

When you want more of God in your life . . .

- 2 CORINTHIANS 3:16-18 | Whenever someone turns to the Lord, the veil is taken away. For the Lord is the Spirit, and wherever the Spirit of the Lord is, there is freedom. So all of us who have had that veil removed can see and reflect the glory of the Lord. And the Lord—who is the Spirit—makes us more and more like him as we are changed into his glorious image.

- PSALM 111:10 | Fear of the LORD is the foundation of true wisdom. All who obey his commandments will grow in wisdom.

- JEREMIAH 15:16 | When I discovered your words, I devoured them. They are my joy and my heart's delight, for I bear your name, O LORD God of Heaven's Armies.

- 2 TIMOTHY 3:16 | All Scripture is inspired by God and is useful to teach us what is true and to make us realize what is wrong in our lives. It corrects us when we are wrong and teaches us to do what is right.

When God seems uninvolved in the world . . .

- MATTHEW 1:23 | Look! The virgin will conceive a child! She will give birth to a son, and they will call him Immanuel, which means "God is with us."

- 1 JOHN 4:9-10 | God showed how much he loved us by sending his one and only Son into the world so that we might have eternal life through him. This is real love— not that we loved God, but that he loved us and sent his Son as a sacrifice to take away our sins.

- JOHN 1:14 | The Word became human and made his home among us. He was full of unfailing love and faithfulness. And we have seen his glory, the glory of the Father's one and only Son.

When you wonder if God wants a relationship with you . . .

- PSALM 27:8 | My heart has heard you say, "Come and talk with me." And my heart responds, "LORD, I am coming."

- PSALM 23:6 | Surely your goodness and unfailing love will pursue me all the days of my life, and I will live in the house of the LORD forever.

When you wonder if your child is capable of a relationship with God . . .

- 1 JOHN 3:1 | See how very much our Father loves us, for he calls us his children, and that is what we are!

- PSALM 24:1 | The earth is the LORD's, and everything in it. The world and all its people belong to him.

- MARK 10:14 | When Jesus saw what was happening, he was angry with his disciples. He said to them, "Let the children come to me. Don't stop them! For the Kingdom of God belongs to those who are like these children."

The best news in the world is that God is always available. God is not only involved in the world, but he is actively pursuing you and your child with goodness and a love that never fails. Your relationship with Jesus gives you the means to connect with God at any time. In his presence you belong; your child belongs. God is with you through every therapy session, every medical emergency, every school meeting, every meltdown, and all the moments of your day.

PRESSURE

When people push you to do more for your child . . .

- PSALM 3:3 | You, O LORD, are a shield around me; you are my glory, the one who holds my head high.

- PSALM 146:3, 5 | Don't put your confidence in powerful people; there is no help for you there. . . . But joyful are those who have the God of Israel as their helper, whose hope is in the LORD their God.

- PSALM 138:8 | The LORD will work out his plans for my life.

When you feel pressure to compromise your values . . .

- PSALM 1:1 | Oh, the joys of those who do not follow the advice of the wicked, or stand around with sinners, or join in with mockers.

- PSALM 25:8 | The LORD is good and does what is right; he shows the proper path to those who go astray.

When you feel crushed by the demands of life . . .

- PSALM 146:8 | The LORD lifts up those who are weighed down. The LORD loves the godly.

- MATTHEW 11:28 | Then Jesus said, "Come to me, all of you who are weary and carry heavy burdens, and I will give you rest."

As the parent of a child with special needs, you may experience pressure all the time. Whether people push you to try a new diet or a new therapy, coping with the pressures of living under stress can paralyze you and make you feel trapped. God reminds you that you can shed those burdens and walk peacefully with him. He will reveal his best plan moment by moment as you look to him for help.

PROVISION
When there isn't enough to give your child what he needs . . .

- PSALM 34:9-10 | Fear the LORD, you his godly people, for those who fear him will have all they need. Even strong young lions sometimes go hungry, but those who trust in the LORD will lack no good thing.

- PHILIPPIANS 4:19 | This same God who takes care of me will supply all your needs from his glorious riches, which have been given to us in Christ Jesus.

When you feel inadequate as a parent . . .

- 2 PETER 1:3 | By his divine power, God has given us everything we need for living a godly life. We have received all of this by coming to know him, the one who called us to himself by means of his marvelous glory and excellence.

- JOHN 15:5 | Yes, I am the vine; you are the branches. Those who remain in me, and I in them, will produce much fruit. For apart from me you can do nothing.

The heartfelt desire of every parent is to provide adequately for the needs of his or her family, but sometimes it's difficult. God knows what your needs are. God loves taking *not enough* and showing how he is *more than enough*. His provisions come from his abundant supply of glorious riches—and you get to be on the receiving end! Where you feel inadequate, God provides the power of his presence with you. You can trust him to provide in times of need.

PURPOSE

When you're searching for fresh enthusiasm in parenting . . .

- PSALM 40:8 | I take joy in doing your will, my God, for your instructions are written on my heart.

When you can't see results and feel like your efforts are useless . . .

- PSALM 57:2 | I cry out to God Most High, to God who will fulfill his purpose for me.

- ACTS 20:24 | My life is worth nothing to me unless I use it for finishing the work assigned me by the Lord Jesus—the work of telling others the Good News about the wonderful grace of God.

- 1 CORINTHIANS 15:58 | So, my dear brothers and sisters, be strong and immovable. Always work enthusiastically for the Lord, for you know that nothing you do for the Lord is ever useless.

When you don't see a reason for your child's special needs . . .

- ROMANS 8:28 | We know that God causes everything to work together for the good of those who love God and are called according to his purpose for them.

- EPHESIANS 1:18 | I pray that your hearts will be flooded with light so that you can understand the confident hope he has given to those he called—his holy people who are his rich and glorious inheritance.

- EPHESIANS 3:10-11 | God's purpose in all this was to use the church to display his wisdom in its rich variety to all the unseen rulers and authorities in the heavenly places. This was his eternal plan, which he carried out through Christ Jesus our Lord.

Living a life full of passion and purpose can seem impossible when you're constantly responding to the urgent needs of your child or others in your family. It's easy to lose focus in the day-to-day because your thoughts are being jerked in so many directions. However, God's purpose for you is simple—love God, love others. In both your daily responsibilities and your sudden emergencies, you can find time to pause and say a quick prayer, asking God to help you respond in a way that honors him and loves others. God wastes nothing, and nothing you do for the Lord is ever useless. The rewards ripple into eternity.

REDEMPTION
When it feels like there must be more to life than this . . .

- EXODUS 15:1, 13 | Moses and the people of Israel sang this song to the LORD: . . . "With your unfailing love you lead the people you have redeemed. In your might, you guide them to your sacred home."

- EPHESIANS 3:20 | All glory to God, who is able, through his mighty power at work within us, to accomplish infinitely more than we might ask or think.

- JOHN 14:12 | I tell you the truth, anyone who believes in me will do the same works I have done, and even greater works, because I am going to be with the Father.

When you feel there's no way to make up for your mistakes . . .

- 2 CORINTHIANS 8:9 | You know the generous grace of our Lord Jesus Christ. Though he was rich, yet for your sakes he became poor, so that by his poverty he could make you rich.

- ISAIAH 44:22 | I have swept away your sins like a cloud. I have scattered your offenses like the morning mist. Oh, return to me, for I have paid the price to set you free.

When you hope God will make things right . . .

- PSALM 103:2-5 | Let all that I am praise the LORD; may I never forget the good things he does for me. He forgives all my sins and heals all my diseases. He redeems me from death and crowns me with love and tender mercies. He fills my life with good things. My youth is renewed like the eagle's!

- ROMANS 8:18 | What we suffer now is nothing compared to the glory he will reveal to us later.

Any parent who has ever watched his or her child suffer knows this world isn't as it should be. Have you ever wished your child or your family could have escaped some of the struggles you've faced through special needs? That desire for things to be made right is the foundation of your hope for redemption. No matter what mistakes you've made, no matter how messed up your life might seem, there is nothing God cannot redeem into something beautiful and meaningful. He has paid the price for every mess in all of creation. And while you wait for heaven to come, you have assurance that God is working for good on your behalf.

REFRESHMENT
When you're looking for a source of new joy . . .

- PSALM 73:26 | My health may fail, and my spirit may grow weak, but God remains the strength of my heart; he is mine forever.

When your soul is weary . . .

- PSALM 119:50 | Your promise revives me; it comforts me in all my troubles.

- PSALM 19:7-8 | The instructions of the LORD are perfect, reviving the soul. . . . The commandments of the LORD are right, bringing joy to the heart.

When your mind is weary . . .

- PSALM 94:19 | When doubts filled my mind, your comfort gave me renewed hope and cheer.

- PSALM 121:4; 124:8 | Indeed, he who watches over Israel never slumbers or sleeps. . . . Our help is from the LORD, who made heaven and earth.

When you lack the energy to do what's right . . .

- ISAIAH 57:15 | The high and lofty one who lives in eternity, the Holy One, says this: "I live in the high and holy place with those whose spirits are contrite and humble. I restore the crushed spirit of the humble and revive the courage of those with repentant hearts."

- PHILIPPIANS 4:13 | I can do everything through Christ, who gives me strength.

- PHILIPPIANS 2:13 | God is working in you, giving you the desire and the power to do what pleases him.

When you want your presence to be refreshing to others . . .

- PROVERBS 11:25 | The generous will prosper; those who refresh others will themselves be refreshed.

- COLOSSIANS 3:10 | Put on your new nature, and be renewed as you learn to know your Creator and become like him.

- GALATIANS 5:22-23 | The Holy Spirit produces this kind of fruit in our lives: love, joy, peace, patience, kindness, goodness, faithfulness, gentleness, and self-control.

Weary. Tired. Worn out. Do those words describe you? You probably shoulder great demands every day, whether through parenting, caregiving, working, or just the never-ending assortment of tasks that fill your hours. Over the long haul, that can leave you feeling exhausted. Though your energy runs out, God's never does. His presence fills you with new strength and joy. His Word refreshes your thoughts each day. His power can well up in you until his refreshing presence replenishes you and spills out on those around you.

REJECTION

When your family members keep their distance . . .

- PSALM 27:10 | Even if my father and mother abandon me, the LORD will hold me close.

- ISAIAH 49:15 | Can a mother forget her nursing child? Can she feel no love for the child she has borne? But even if that were possible, I would not forget you!

When your friends leave you out . . .

- PSALM 25:14 | The LORD is a friend to those who fear him. He teaches them his covenant.

- ROMANS 5:11 | Now we can rejoice in our wonderful new relationship with God because our Lord Jesus Christ has made us friends of God.

When your child is never invited . . .

- ISAIAH 64:4-5 | Since the world began, no ear has heard and no eye has seen a God like you, who works for those who wait for him! You welcome those who gladly do good, who follow godly ways.

- PSALM 37:18 | Day by day the LORD takes care of the innocent, and they will receive an inheritance that lasts forever.

When rejection hurts . . .

- PSALM 34:22 | The LORD will redeem those who serve him. No one who takes refuge in him will be condemned.

When people just can't understand your family's needs . . .

- MATTHEW 6:8 | Your Father knows exactly what you need even before you ask him!

- PSALM 33:13-15 | The LORD looks down from heaven and sees the whole human race. From his throne he observes all who live on the earth. He made their hearts, so he understands everything they do.

When it feels like even God has cast you aside . . .

- PSALM 51:17 | The sacrifice you desire is a broken spirit. You will not reject a broken and repentant heart, O God.

- PSALM 94:14 | The LORD will not reject his people; he will not abandon his special possession.

- JOHN 6:37 | Those the Father has given me will come to me, and I will never reject them.

Have you felt cast aside since your child's special needs were identified? Have you felt left out because people don't understand your family? We all experience feelings of rejection sometimes. It hurts when you need support and connection but instead receive distance and a cold shoulder. Dealing with rejection isn't easy, and it can make you feel isolated. In these times, it is helpful to cling to the truth that God hasn't forgotten you. He is your safe place and a welcoming presence. God promises that he already knows your needs. He welcomes both you and your child into close relationship with him.

RENEWAL
When you're desperate for something to change . . .

- 2 CORINTHIANS 5:17 | Anyone who belongs to Christ has become a new person. The old life is gone; a new life has begun!

- REVELATION 21:5 | The one sitting on the throne said, "Look, I am making everything new!"

When you're too exhausted to think . . .

- PSALM 36:9 | You are the fountain of life, the light by which we see.

When you feel spiritually dull and indifferent . . .

- EZEKIEL 36:26 | I will give you a new heart, and I will put a new spirit in you. I will take out your stony, stubborn heart and give you a tender, responsive heart.

- PSALM 126:4-6 | Restore our fortunes, LORD, as streams renew the desert. Those who plant in tears will harvest with shouts of joy. They weep as they go to plant their seed, but they sing as they return with the harvest.

- EPHESIANS 2:1, 4-5 | Once you were dead because of your disobedience and your many sins. . . . But God is so rich in mercy, and he loved us so much, that even though we were dead because of our sins, he gave us life when he raised Christ from the dead.

When you need to rekindle your marriage . . .

- COLOSSIANS 3:14 | Above all, clothe yourselves with love, which binds us all together in perfect harmony.

- JOHN 15:12-13 | Love each other in the same way I have loved you. There is no greater love than to lay down one's life for one's friends.

The demands of being a special needs parent can lead to burnout, causing both spiritual and relational apathy. Do you ever find yourself longing to escape your life or your responsibilities? This may be a sign that you are in need of spiritual resuscitation. God promises that a new life begins when you first become a Christian, and that process of renewal continues throughout your whole lifetime. God's energy and creativity are like a fountain that continually pours out new life into your heart and spirit as you trust him. If you're looking for a change, first surrender your heart to Christ. He is the source of everything new.

RESPITE

When you need a break from the world of special needs . . .

- PSALM 32:7 | You are my hiding place.

- PSALM 23:1-2 | The LORD is my shepherd. . . . He lets me rest in green meadows; he leads me beside peaceful streams.

When there's no end in sight . . .

- HEBREWS 4:9 | There is a special rest still waiting for the people of God.

Do you ever wish you could take a break from everything special needs and just be a regular parent? It's okay to feel that way, and it might even indicate that your heart is in need of some rest and recovery. God hasn't reserved rest only for some and not for you. In whatever way you can get a break, it's important to take some time to refresh your body and mind. If you can't leave your child in another's care, ask God to guide you in finding respites in the schedule you have. He is your getaway place, your guiding Shepherd. Little moments of respite might be just what you need to enjoy your new normal.

REST
When you're tired of being tired . . .

- JEREMIAH 31:25 | I have given rest to the weary and joy to the sorrowing.

- MATTHEW 11:28 | Jesus said, "Come to me, all of you who are weary and carry heavy burdens, and I will give you rest."

When you have trouble slowing down . . .

- PSALM 116:7 | Let my soul be at rest again, for the LORD has been good to me.

- PSALM 62:1-2 | I wait quietly before God, for my victory comes from him. He alone is my rock and my salvation, my fortress where I will never be shaken.

- HEBREWS 4:10 | All who have entered into God's rest have rested from their labors, just as God did after creating the world.

Rest may seem like a luxury you cannot afford as a parent of a child with special needs. Constantly trying to stay on top of the needs of your child and your family leaves little room for leisure and relaxation. Yet if God, who is unlimited in power, rested after his creation work, your limited body and spirit especially need rest. Rest is God's design so you can experience his goodness and find reprieve from weariness. Resting honors the way God made you and refreshes your body and spirit so you can enjoy your child and your family.

SACRIFICE

When you have to give up your dreams to care for your child . . .

- HEBREWS 13:16 | Don't forget to do good and to share with those in need. These are the sacrifices that please God.

- EPHESIANS 5:2 | Live a life filled with love, following the example of Christ. He loved us and offered himself as a sacrifice for us, a pleasing aroma to God.

- MATTHEW 16:25 | If you try to hang on to your life, you will lose it. But if you give up your life for my sake, you will save it.

When you don't know how much more you can give . . .

- GALATIANS 2:20 | My old self has been crucified with Christ. It is no longer I who live, but Christ lives in me. So I live in this earthly body by trusting in the Son of God, who loved me and gave himself for me.

- 2 CORINTHIANS 12:9 | Each time he said, "My grace is all you need. My power works best in weakness."

When you forget what God has given up for you . . .

- GALATIANS 1:4 | Jesus gave his life for our sins, just as God our Father planned, in order to rescue us from this evil world in which we live.

- 1 PETER 2:24 | He personally carried our sins in his body on the cross so that we can be dead to sin and live for what is right. By his wounds you are healed.

- JOHN 3:16 | This is how God loved the world: He gave his one and only Son, so that everyone who believes in him will not perish but have eternal life.

When you give thanks through the pain . . .

- PSALM 50:23 | Giving thanks is a sacrifice that truly honors me. If you keep to my path, I will reveal to you the salvation of God.

- PSALM 50:14-15 | Make thankfulness your sacrifice to God, and keep the vows you made to the Most High. Then call on me when you are in trouble, and I will rescue you, and you will give me glory.

When you feel resentful of how much you give up for your child . . .

- JAMES 5:8-9 | You, too, must be patient. Take courage, for the coming of the Lord is near. Don't grumble about each other, brothers and sisters, or you will be judged. For look—the Judge is standing at the door!

- GALATIANS 6:9 | Let's not get tired of doing what is good. At just the right time we will reap a harvest of blessing if we don't give up.

- ISAIAH 26:3 | You will keep in perfect peace all who trust in you, all whose thoughts are fixed on you!

When you let go of what you want to follow Jesus . . .

- ROMANS 12:1-2 | So, dear brothers and sisters, I plead with you to give your bodies to God because of all he has done for you. Let them be a living and holy sacrifice—the kind he will find acceptable. This is truly the way to worship him. Don't copy the behavior and customs of this world, but let God transform you into a new person by changing the way you

think. Then you will learn to know God's will for
you, which is good and pleasing and perfect.

A sacrifice is when you give up something for the greater
good. Sometimes when you're parenting a child with special
needs, it's easy to give up everything for your child. At other
times, it can be painful to continue to give and give when it
feels like the returns are minimal. Jesus gave up his life—the
ultimate sacrifice—for you and for your child. He knows
what it is to sacrifice, and he sees you. Not one thing you give
in this life goes unnoticed. Whatever you give up for the sake
of Jesus will be returned with extra blessings. Make sure to
check your attitude and your heart. When you feel bitterness
and resentment sneaking in, it may be a sign that you need a
fresh reminder of what God gave out of love for you.

SAFETY

*When your child's emotional instability puts you on
edge . . .*

- PROVERBS 15:1 | A gentle answer deflects anger, but
  harsh words make tempers flare.

- PROVERBS 1:33 | All who listen to me will live in peace,
  untroubled by fear of harm.

- PSALM 26:8, 12 | I love your sanctuary, LORD, the place where your glorious presence dwells. . . . Now I stand on solid ground, and I will publicly praise the LORD.

When you don't feel safe in your own home . . .

- PSALM 90:1 | Lord, through all the generations you have been our home!

- PSALM 62:8 | O my people, trust in him at all times. Pour out your heart to him, for God is our refuge.

- PSALM 75:3 | When the earth quakes and its people live in turmoil, I am the one who keeps its foundations firm.

When others make you feel insecure . . .

- PSALM 37:28 | The LORD loves justice, and he will never abandon the godly. He will keep them safe forever.

- DEUTERONOMY 33:3 | [God] loves his people; all his holy ones are in his hands.

- PROVERBS 19:23 | Fear of the LORD leads to life, bringing security and protection from harm.

When you wonder if your child can take care of himself. . .

- PSALM 25:8 | The LORD is good and does what is right; he shows the proper path to those who go astray.

- PSALM 32:10 | Unfailing love surrounds those who trust the LORD.

When your child has special challenges or thinks about the world differently, it is easy to worry about his or her safety. Maybe you even find yourself worried for your own safety or that of your family members. God has comforting words for you when you or your child is threatened or feels insecure. First, you are not facing this alone. God stands by you and surrounds you with his unfailing protection. When your surroundings don't seem safe, God invites you to take refuge in him, to make yourself at home in his presence. Ask for his guidance if you need to determine when to seek outside help. Whether it is your emotions of insecurity or your child's that you are dealing with, the Lord assures you that you will have peace when you decide to trust in his promises more than in what you see. For those who follow Jesus, safety is already guaranteed in heaven. Perhaps you need the courage to seek some help or to persevere through a threatening situation. Let these promises provide you with confidence to move forward, knowing that you and your child are in the protective care of your loving God.

SHAME

When you are mortified at your child's diagnosis . . .

- 2 THESSALONIANS 3:16 | May the Lord of peace himself give you his peace at all times and in every situation. The Lord be with you all.

- PSALM 86:5 | O Lord, you are so good, so ready to forgive, so full of unfailing love for all who ask for your help.

When the enemy accuses and makes you feel you're to blame . . .

- PSALM 25:1-3 | O LORD, I give my life to you. I trust in you, my God! Do not let me be disgraced, or let my enemies rejoice in my defeat. No one who trusts in you will ever be disgraced, but disgrace comes to those who try to deceive others.

- EPHESIANS 4:21-24 | Since you have heard about Jesus and have learned the truth that comes from him, throw off your old sinful nature and your former way of life, which is corrupted by lust and deception. Instead, let the Spirit renew your thoughts and attitudes. Put on your new nature, created to be like God—truly righteous and holy.

When you want to take the high road . . .

- PSALM 34:5 | Those who look to him for help will be radiant with joy; no shadow of shame will darken their faces.

- EPHESIANS 5:7-9 | Don't participate in the things these people do. For once you were full of darkness, but now you have light from the Lord. So live as people of light! For this light within you produces only what is good and right and true.

It can be distressing to you as a parent when your child is identified as having special needs. You might experience a deep sense of loss or even feel that your typical family ways have been threatened. You may worry about what people will think of you or your child. When dealing with feelings of shame, it's easy for lies to creep into your mind. Any message that tells you it's all your fault, it's beyond hope, or you should feel deep shame about who your child is—is not from God. Don't let yourself be dragged down into the darkness of shame and regret. Check your mind daily with Scripture, and let God replace thoughts of guilt with thoughts of grace. You need a daily reminder that you belong to God and you and your child are loved by him. This is the way to live joyfully above your circumstances, free of shame and guilt.

SPECIAL

When you wonder what makes your child special . . .

- GENESIS 1:27 | God created human beings in his own image. In the image of God he created them; male and female he created them.

- DEUTERONOMY 26:18 | The LORD has declared today that you are his people, his own special treasure, just as he promised.

- 1 CORINTHIANS 12:7 | A spiritual gift is given to each of us so we can help each other.

- EPHESIANS 2:10 | We are God's masterpiece. He has created us anew in Christ Jesus, so we can do the good things he planned for us long ago.

Your child isn't special because of her special needs, although it certainly makes her unique. Your child is special because she was created by a loving God in his very likeness with dignity and great worth because she is known and loved by him. She is special because God designed her body and her personality both to reflect him and to give him honor. One of the greatest gifts you can give your child is to help her see that she is special and of great worth in God's eyes.

❖

SPECIAL DIETS

When your whole family has to sacrifice for the sake of your child's dietary needs . . .

- HEBREWS 13:16 | Don't forget to do good and to share with those in need. These are the sacrifices that please God.

When special diets seem to steal away your enjoyment of food . . .

- PSALM 34:8-10 | Taste and see that the LORD is good. Oh, the joys of those who take refuge in him! Fear the LORD, you his godly people, for those who fear him will have all they need. Even strong young lions sometimes go hungry, but those who trust in the LORD will lack no good thing.

- PSALM 23:5 | You prepare a feast for me in the presence of my enemies. . . . My cup overflows with blessings.

When a special diet seems overwhelming . . .

- HEBREWS 13:8-9 | Jesus Christ is the same yesterday, today, and forever. . . . Your strength comes from God's grace, not from rules about food.

- PSALM 145:15-16 | The eyes of all look to you in hope; you give them their food as they need it. When you open your hand, you satisfy the hunger and thirst of every living thing.

Perhaps your child has allergies to many foods or has a limited diet because of health concerns or personal preferences. Regardless of the reason, changing the way you eat and think about food is difficult. God knows the level at which you sacrifice for your children, and he is pleased when you make sacrifices for their good. Though your diet may change, he promises that he is always the same. He is your source of strength and deepest satisfaction.

STRENGTH
When you need to be strong . . .

- PSALM 138:3 | As soon as I pray, you answer me; you encourage me by giving me strength.

When you feel like you're not strong enough to parent a child with special needs . . .

- EPHESIANS 3:16-17 | I pray that from his glorious, unlimited resources he will empower you with inner strength through his Spirit. Then Christ will make his home in your hearts as you trust in him. Your roots will grow down into God's love and keep you strong.

When you feel like you're not up for the task at hand . . .

- 2 SAMUEL 22:40 | You have armed me with strength for the battle.

- PSALM 18:28-29 | You light a lamp for me. The LORD, my God, lights up my darkness. In your strength I can crush an army; with my God I can scale any wall.

- PSALM 73:26 | My health may fail, and my spirit may grow weak, but God remains the strength of my heart; he is mine forever.

Some days you may not feel up to the task of meeting your child's needs. There can be many reasons why your strength fails you or your soul is discouraged. When your physical strength is gone and your willpower gives out, God has promised to give you the strength you lack. His resources are unlimited, and he is by your side, helping you fight your battles and giving you strength to keep going.

STRESS

When your mind is buzzing with worry . . .

- MATTHEW 6:31-32 | Don't worry about these things, saying, "What will we eat? What will we drink? What will we wear?" These things dominate the thoughts of unbelievers, but your heavenly Father already knows all your needs.

- ISAIAH 26:3 | You will keep in perfect peace all who trust in you, all whose thoughts are fixed on you!

When your child's therapists or doctors pressure you to do more . . .

- PSALM 55:22 | Give your burdens to the LORD, and he will take care of you. He will not permit the godly to slip and fall.

When anxiety keeps you up at night . . .

- PSALM 127:2 | It is useless for you to work so hard from early morning until late at night, anxiously working . . . for God gives rest to his loved ones.

- PROVERBS 3:21-22, 24 | My child, don't lose sight of common sense and discernment. Hang on to them, for they will refresh your soul. . . . You can go to bed without fear; you will lie down and sleep soundly.

When you struggle to cope with the weight of your child's needs . . .

- 2 CORINTHIANS 1:8-9 | We were crushed and over-whelmed beyond our ability to endure, and we thought we would never live through it. In fact, we expected to die. But as a result, we stopped relying on ourselves and learned to rely only on God, who raises the dead.

- PSALM 94:18-19 | I cried out, "I am slipping!" but your unfailing love, O LORD, supported me. When doubts filled my mind, your comfort gave me renewed hope and cheer.

When your child's needs feel like a tangled web of issues and you don't know how to start unraveling them . . .

- ISAIAH 45:18 | The LORD is God, and he created the heavens and earth and put everything in place. He made the world to be lived in, not to be a place of empty chaos. "I am the LORD," he says, "and there is no other."

- PSALM 86:7 | I will call to you whenever I'm in trouble, and you will answer me.

- PSALM 37:23 | The LORD directs the steps of the godly. He delights in every detail of their lives.

Do you carry an incredible weight on your shoulders? Do you have days when you feel like you might break under the pressure of parenting a child with special needs? Do you lie awake at night with anxious thoughts or find yourself fretting about things beyond your control? It's amazing how stress can both paralyze you and keep you spinning. God's promises are for times like these. He knows what you need before you ask. He will take care of you. God offers peace and rest. These aren't just inspirational sayings—they are the forever promises God makes to those who trust him. Fix your thoughts on who God is and his promises. This allows his peace to settle your heart and mind and keep you from crumbling under the pressure.

STRUGGLE

When everyday tasks take exponentially longer with your child . . .

- ECCLESIASTES 3:10-11 | I have seen the burden God has placed on us all. Yet God has made everything beautiful for its own time. He has planted eternity in the human heart, but even so, people cannot see the whole scope of God's work from beginning to end.

- COLOSSIANS 1:11 | We also pray that you will be strengthened with all his glorious power so you will have all the endurance and patience you need.

When working with your child to develop a new skill is hard, and you want to pull your hair out . . .

- JAMES 5:7-8 | Dear brothers and sisters, be patient as you wait for the Lord's return. Consider the farmers who patiently wait for the rains in the fall and in the spring. They eagerly look for the valuable harvest to ripen. You, too, must be patient. Take courage, for the coming of the Lord is near.

- ECCLESIASTES 7:8 | Finishing is better than starting. Patience is better than pride.

- ZECHARIAH 4:10 | Do not despise these small beginnings, for the LORD rejoices to see the work begin.

When you feel like you're constantly behind in life . . .

- 2 CORINTHIANS 4:18 | We don't look at the troubles we can see now; rather, we fix our gaze on things that cannot be seen. For the things we see now will soon be gone, but the things we cannot see will last forever.

- PHILIPPIANS 3:12, 14 | I don't mean to say that I have already achieved these things or that I have already reached perfection. . . . I press on to reach the end of the race and receive the heavenly prize for which God, through Christ Jesus, is calling us.

There are seasons of struggle in everyone's life, and parents of children with special needs are no exception. In these times, everyday activities can feel like great burdens, and beginning something new can feel like an impossible feat. You may question whether anything will ever come easily or you'll ever catch a break. As you go through seasons of struggle, hold on to God's promises of future stability. Rest, peace, and security are his end goals, and he will walk you and your child there. Let his promises be the lens through which you view your struggles. When you are lacking is when God provides.

STUMBLE
When the next steps are uncertain . . .

- PSALM 119:165 | Those who love your instructions have great peace and do not stumble.

- HOSEA 14:9 | Let those who are wise understand these things. Let those with discernment listen carefully. The paths of the LORD are true and right, and righteous people live by walking in them. But in those paths sinners stumble and fall.

When you're afraid you've gone in the wrong direction . . .

- PSALM 18:33, 36 | He makes me as surefooted as a deer, enabling me to stand on mountain heights. . . . You have made a wide path for my feet to keep them from slipping.

- PSALM 3:3 | You, O LORD, are a shield around me; you are my glory, the one who holds my head high.

So many voices vie for your attention as a special needs parent. Some offer encouragement to try this therapy or that diet or some new intervention. Others give advice about how to raise kids and shape their faith and character. It's no wonder parents sometimes flounder and stumble. There are so many directions, but which way is best? When you walk with the Lord, he guides your steps today so that you won't slip tomorrow. His presence keeps you on the best path for you and your child.

SUFFERING

When you wonder how you're going to make it through this trial . . .

- 2 CORINTHIANS 1:21-22 | It is God who enables us, along with you, to stand firm for Christ. He has commissioned us, and he has identified us as his own by placing the Holy Spirit in our hearts as the first installment that guarantees everything he has promised us.

- PSALM 22:24 | He has not ignored or belittled the suffering of the needy. He has not turned his back on them, but has listened to their cries for help.

- ISAIAH 43:1-2 | Listen to the LORD who created you. . . . The one who formed you says, "Do not be afraid, for I have ransomed you. I have called you by name; you are mine. When you go through deep waters, I will be with you. When you go through rivers of difficulty, you will not drown. When you walk through the fire of oppression, you will not be burned up; the flames will not consume you."

When your suffering feels pointless . . .

- 2 CORINTHIANS 4:10 | Through suffering, our bodies continue to share in the death of Jesus so that the life of Jesus may also be seen in our bodies.

- 1 PETER 4:12-13 | Dear friends, don't be surprised at the fiery trials you are going through, as if something strange were happening to you. Instead, be very glad—for these trials make you partners with Christ in his suffering, so that you will have the wonderful joy of seeing his glory when it is revealed to all the world.

When you wonder if anyone notices the burdens you carry . . .

- PSALM 56:8 | You keep track of all my sorrows. You have collected all my tears in your bottle. You have recorded each one in your book.

- ISAIAH 49:13 | The LORD has comforted his people and will have compassion on them in their suffering.

When you wonder if it will ever stop hurting . . .

- JAMES 5:10-11 | For examples of patience in suffering, dear brothers and sisters, look at the prophets who spoke in the name of the Lord. We give great honor to those who endure under suffering. For instance, you know about Job, a man of great endurance. You can see how the Lord was kind to him at the end, for the Lord is full of tenderness and mercy.

- 1 PETER 5:10 | In his kindness God called you to share in his eternal glory by means of Christ Jesus. So after you have suffered a little while, he will restore, support, and strengthen you, and he will place you on a firm foundation.

When your child is suffering . . .

- PSALM 103:17-18 | The love of the LORD remains forever with those who fear him. His salvation extends to the children's children of those who are faithful to his covenant, of those who obey his commandments!

- 2 CORINTHIANS 1:3 | God is our merciful Father and the source of all comfort.

- PSALM 102:27-28 | You are always the same; you will live forever. The children of your people will live in security. Their children's children will thrive in your presence.

- ISAIAH 46:4 | I will be your God throughout your lifetime—until your hair is white with age. I made you, and I will care for you. I will carry you along and save you.

- ISAIAH 63:9 | In all their suffering he also suffered, and he personally rescued them. In his love and mercy he redeemed them. He lifted them up and carried them through all the years.

When you're in the midst of a season of suffering, it can seem like your struggles will go on and on. It is easy to get discouraged and even despair, especially when you have to watch a loved one go through pain. God promises that suffering is for a season, though for some that season could be much of their time on this earth. But even that length of time is short compared to living with full health for all of eternity. In the meantime, let God, who promises eternal freedom from suffering, be your primary source of comfort, for he cares deeply about all your pain. You may not understand why bad things happen in your life, but you can still have confidence that God is with you and is supporting you in the midst of them. If you are hurting, hold on to him. If your child is suffering, point him or her to Jesus, the source of comfort.

SUPPORT
When you need someone to lean on . . .

- LAMENTATIONS 3:25 | The LORD is good to those who depend on him, to those who search for him.

When God feels impersonal and you wonder if he can really help . . .

- ISAIAH 41:10 | Don't be afraid, for I am with you. Don't be discouraged, for I am your God. I will strengthen you and help you. I will hold you up with my victorious right hand.

When you're exhausted from fighting for your child and wish someone would stand up for you . . .

- DEUTERONOMY 33:27 | The eternal God is your refuge, and his everlasting arms are under you.

He drives out the enemy before you; he cries out,
"Destroy them!"

They say it takes a village to raise a child. For a child with
special needs, it can take an army! You need support. It is
important to have people you can lean on, but ultimately,
God is the one you can depend on most. He is sovereign
over you and your child. He isn't uninvolved but is deeply
concerned about the battles you fight on a daily basis. The
support you have and will have are ultimately blessings from
a God who is holding you and your child. You can face
today boldly and be encouraged because the Lord is the
foundation of your support system.

SURVIVAL
When you wonder how you've survived this long . . .

- 1 CORINTHIANS 15:10 | Whatever I am now, it is all
  because God poured out his special favor on me—and
  not without results. For I have worked harder than any
  of the other apostles; yet it was not I but God who was
  working through me by his grace.

When people tell you they could never do what you do . . .

- PSALM 36:7 | How precious is your unfailing love, O God! All humanity finds shelter in the shadow of your wings.

- PSALM 40:1 | I waited patiently for the LORD to help me, and he turned to me and heard my cry.

- PSALM 3:3 | You, O LORD, are a shield around me; you are my glory, the one who holds my head high.

When it seems like your whole life is lived in survival mode . . .

- PSALM 34:19 | The righteous person faces many troubles, but the LORD comes to the rescue each time.

- ISAIAH 30:15 | Only in returning to me and resting in me will you be saved. In quietness and confidence is your strength.

When you long to thrive instead of survive . . .

- JOSHUA 1:7 | Be strong and very courageous. Be careful to obey. . . . Do not deviate . . . to the right or to the left. Then you will be successful in everything you do.

- JOSHUA 1:8 | Study this Book of Instruction continually.
  Meditate on it day and night so you will be sure to obey
  everything written in it. Only then will you prosper and
  succeed in all you do.

- DEUTERONOMY 11:18-21 | Commit yourselves whole-
  heartedly to these words of mine. Tie them to your
  hands and wear them on your forehead as reminders.
  Teach them to your children. Talk about them when
  you are at home and when you are on the road, when
  you are going to bed and when you are getting up.
  Write them on the doorposts of your house and on your
  gates, so that as long as the sky remains above the earth,
  you and your children may flourish in the land the
  LORD swore to give your ancestors.

- PSALM 92:12-14 | The godly will flourish like palm
  trees and grow strong like the cedars of Lebanon. For they
  are transplanted to the LORD's own house. They flourish
  in the courts of our God. Even in old age they will still
  produce fruit; they will remain vital and green.

Do you ever feel like you're just surviving? Just barely holding
on? Do you feel like you're in a pattern of only responding to
the emergencies of your child and your family? That's survival
mode. You can sustain it for a time, but not forever. It can hurt,
too, when others say they could never live the life you're living
because at times, you may feel like you can't either! God's intention is for his people to thrive, not in the absence of difficulty,

but in spite of difficulty. Trusting God is the foundation of a flourishing life, enabling you to have peace in the midst of pain, love others when none is returned, and serve even while you suffer. The ability to do anything well comes by the grace of God. By following him and trusting in his grace there can be fruit in every season, even survival mode.

TEARS

When you cry alone . . .

- PSALM 18:6 | In my distress I cried out to the LORD; yes, I prayed to my God for help. He heard me from his sanctuary; my cry to him reached his ears.

- ISAIAH 38:5 | This is what the LORD, the God of your ancestor David, says: "I have heard your prayer and seen your tears."

When the tears flow freely . . .

- PSALM 30:5 | Weeping may last through the night, but joy comes with the morning.

- PSALM 56:8 | You keep track of all my sorrows. You have collected all my tears in your bottle. You have recorded each one in your book.

When your work is saturated with sadness . . .

- PSALM 126:4-6 | Restore our fortunes, LORD, as streams renew the desert. Those who plant in tears will harvest with shouts of joy. They weep as they go to plant their seed, but they sing as they return with the harvest.

When you weep with regret . . .

- PSALM 116:7-9 | Let my soul be at rest again, for the LORD has been good to me. He has saved me from death, my eyes from tears, my feet from stumbling. And so I walk in the LORD's presence as I live here on earth!

Maybe you find yourself making decisions through tears or working hard and pushing through in distress. It's okay to cry. Your tears are precious to God whether they are tears of sorrow or repentance. Sometimes your sad days seem to go on and on. Deep sorrow can make you feel isolated from others, even God. God promises that even if there is not another soul to cry with, he sees your tears and hears your prayers. Prayer is a great way to shed light on the reasons for your sadness and be reminded that you are not alone when you are with God. Your soul can find rest again in closeness with him.

TEMPTATION

When a particular sin has a hold on you . . .

- GALATIANS 5:16 | Let the Holy Spirit guide your lives. Then you won't be doing what your sinful nature craves.

- ROMANS 8:5-6 | Those who are dominated by the sinful nature think about sinful things, but those who are controlled by the Holy Spirit think about things that please the Spirit. So letting your sinful nature control your mind leads to death. But letting the Spirit control your mind leads to life and peace.

- PROVERBS 5:21-23 | The LORD sees clearly what a man does, examining every path he takes. An evil man is held captive by his own sins; they are ropes that catch and hold him. He will die for lack of self-control; he will be lost because of his great foolishness.

- 1 PETER 5:8 | Stay alert! Watch out for your great enemy, the devil. He prowls around like a roaring lion, looking for someone to devour.

When anger or pain makes you feel entitled to do what you want . . .

- JAMES 1:13-15 | Remember, when you are being tempted, do not say, "God is tempting me." God is never tempted to do wrong, and he never tempts anyone else. Temptation comes from our own desires, which entice us and drag us away. These desires give birth to sinful actions. And when sin is allowed to grow, it gives birth to death.

When you're afraid there's no way out except to just give in . . .

- JAMES 1:12 | God blesses those who patiently endure testing and temptation. Afterward they will receive the crown of life that God has promised to those who love him.

- 2 CHRONICLES 19:11 | Take courage as you fulfill your duties, and may the LORD be with those who do what is right.

- PSALM 62:1 | I wait quietly before God, for my victory comes from him.

- MARK 14:38 | Keep watch and pray, so that you will not give in to temptation. For the spirit is willing, but the body is weak.

When it feels like no one understands your battle . . .

- HEBREWS 2:18 | Since he himself has gone through suffering and testing, he is able to help us when we are being tested.

When you need to know God will save you from this . . .

- 1 CORINTHIANS 10:13 | The temptations in your life are no different from what others experience. And God is faithful. He will not allow the temptation to be more than you can stand. When you are tempted, he will show you a way out so that you can endure.

- 2 THESSALONIANS 3:3 | The Lord is faithful; he will strengthen you and guard you from the evil one.

When you need a strategy to keep your heart faithful . . .

- EPHESIANS 6:10-12 | Be strong in the Lord and in his mighty power. Put on all of God's armor so that you will be able to stand firm against all strategies of the devil. For we are not fighting against flesh-and-blood enemies, but against evil rulers and authorities of the unseen world, against mighty powers in this dark world, and against evil spirits in the heavenly places.

- PSALM 119:11 | I have hidden your word in my heart, that I might not sin against you.

What makes temptation so difficult is that you can't always see it for what it is. God has a plan for your life—but the enemy does too. Your struggles with sin come from a weak or wounded heart that is targeted by an enemy who can make evil plots look like heavenly blessings. You are being fought over, and Jesus wants to fight this battle for you. Only his power can conquer what has a hold on you. Having a hard life doesn't entitle you to extra indulgence. God reminds you that others have the same struggles too. Jesus went through tremendous trials and suffering, and he understands the place you're in right now. Satan wants you to feel like no one understands and that his way is the only way out. When you're facing temptation, train yourself to dive in to God's Word. That will focus your thoughts on what is actually true when your heart wants to tell you otherwise. Finally, know that you are commanded to be strong *in the Lord* and *his* mighty power. Your willpower is no match for the power of the enemy. But God's power has already won the war.

THANKFULNESS
When you count your blessings . . .

- PSALM 50:23 | Giving thanks is a sacrifice that truly honors me. If you keep to my path, I will reveal to you the salvation of God.

- PSALM 92:1 | It is good to give thanks to the LORD, to sing praises to the Most High.

When it's hard to be thankful . . .

- 1 CHRONICLES 16:34 | Give thanks to the LORD, for he is good! His faithful love endures forever.

- PSALM 138:1-2 | I give you thanks, O LORD, with all my heart. . . . I praise your name for your unfailing love and faithfulness; for your promises are backed by all the honor of your name.

- EPHESIANS 2:8 | God saved you by his grace when you believed. And you can't take credit for this; it is a gift from God.

- 1 TIMOTHY 1:12, 14 | I thank Christ Jesus our Lord, who has given me strength to do his work. He considered me trustworthy and appointed me to serve him. . . . He filled me with the faith and love that come from Christ Jesus.

When you want to demonstrate your gratitude to God . . .

- PSALM 119:7 | As I learn your righteous regulations, I will thank you by living as I should!

- 1 THESSALONIANS 5:18 | Be thankful in all circumstances, for this is God's will for you who belong to Christ Jesus.

Gratitude may not come naturally. Your tendency may be to focus on what's lacking in your life rather than on what you already have. That is why the Bible often reminds you how good it is to give thanks. The psalmist even commands himself to be thankful. Giving thanks can be a difficult habit to adopt, but it completely transforms your mind's focus. Instead of seeing your problems, you start seeing God's provisions. As a special needs parent, in a sense you are trained to see the problems with your child's health, development, or behavior. This is all the more reason to practice thanking God for whatever you can each day. When your mind is in a state of abundance, your heart can operate with generosity.

TRIALS
When problem after problem shakes your sense of security . . .

- PSALM 46:1-2 | God is our refuge and strength, always ready to help in times of trouble. So we will not fear when earthquakes come and the mountains crumble into the sea.

- JOHN 16:33 | [Jesus said,] "Here on earth you will have many trials and sorrows. But take heart, because I have overcome the world."

When you wonder how long you can endure . . .

- 2 CORINTHIANS 4:17 | Our present troubles are small and won't last very long. Yet they produce for us a glory that vastly outweighs them and will last forever!

When you need someone to call for help . . .

- PSALM 34:19 | The righteous person faces many troubles, but the LORD comes to the rescue each time.

- PSALM 86:7 | I will call to you whenever I'm in trouble, and you will answer me.

Life is full of trials. Caring for someone with special needs brings many situations your way that can test your patience and endurance. Maybe today's trials include financial stress, meltdowns, exhaustion, a difficult therapy session, or food issues. Sometimes the trials are so intense—like a huge medical setback, the loss of a job, or your child missing another milestone—that you are left feeling vulnerable and insecure. God's promise to you is that he is your strong foundation when your world is shaking. He is always waiting to help you and listening for your call. He promises to be with you now. He knows what you are going through. Whatever the problem, God has already figured it all out. Let the reality of these promises soak deep into your heart to give you new confidence as you face today.

VICTORY

When your child overcomes a major obstacle . . .

- PSALM 20:5 | May we shout for joy when we hear of your victory and raise a victory banner in the name of our God.

- 1 CHRONICLES 16:34 | Give thanks to the LORD, for he is good! His faithful love endures forever.

- PSALM 98:1-2 | Sing a new song to the LORD, for he has done wonderful deeds. His right hand has won a mighty victory; his holy arm has shown his saving power! The LORD has announced his victory and has revealed his righteousness to every nation!

When you stand up for what is right . . .

- PSALM 37:5-6 | Commit everything you do to the LORD. Trust him, and he will help you. He will make your innocence radiate like the dawn, and the justice of your cause will shine like the noonday sun.

When you need a champion . . .

- PSALM 44:3 | They did not conquer the land with their swords; it was not their own strong arm that gave them victory. It was your right hand and strong arm and the blinding light from your face that helped them, for you loved them.

- PSALM 62:7 | My victory and honor come from God alone.

When the blows of life make you feel completely defeated . . .

- ROMANS 8:35-37 | Can anything ever separate us from Christ's love? Does it mean he no longer loves us if we have trouble or calamity, or are persecuted, or hungry, or destitute, or in danger, or threatened with death? (As the Scriptures say, "For your sake we are killed every day; we are being slaughtered like sheep.") No, despite all these things, overwhelming victory is ours through Christ, who loved us.

When you get used to feeling like a loser and need to remember who you are . . .

- REVELATION 17:14 | Together they will go to war against the Lamb, but the Lamb will defeat them because he is Lord of all lords and King of all kings.

And his called and chosen and faithful ones will be with him.

- 1 JOHN 4:4 | You belong to God, my dear children. You have already won a victory over those people, because the Spirit who lives in you is greater than the spirit who lives in the world.

These promises remind you that victory is your life's outcome! Satan, your enemy, wants you to focus on feeling defeated and tries to make you believe defeat is the outcome before you even begin. Nothing is further from the truth. God has already won the ultimate victory over sin and death, and he fights your battles for you daily. In times of both celebration and defeat, it is important to remember that victory comes from the Lord. So thank him for the victories in your life and your child's life. Honor him by seeking his help in prayer during times of trouble. Your strength, and your child's strength, can only accomplish and endure so much. Relying on God's strength will carry you victoriously through anything. Victory is your guarantee because you belong to God.

VULNERABILITY

When it hurts to share your story over and over again . . .

- 2 CORINTHIANS 1:5 | The more we suffer for Christ, the more God will shower us with his comfort through Christ.

When you wonder if it's worth letting people into your heart . . .

- PROVERBS 27:17 | As iron sharpens iron, so a friend sharpens a friend.

- ECCLESIASTES 4:9-12 | Two people are better off than one, for they can help each other succeed. If one person falls, the other can reach out and help. But someone who falls alone is in real trouble. Likewise, two people lying close together can keep each other warm. But how can one be warm alone? A person standing alone can be attacked and defeated, but two can stand back-to-back and conquer. Three are even better, for a triple-braided cord is not easily broken.

When you're afraid to let people into the messiness of your life . . .

- PSALM 25:21 | May integrity and honesty protect me, for I put my hope in you.

- COLOSSIANS 4:5-6 | Live wisely among those who are not believers, and make the most of every opportunity. Let your conversation be gracious and attractive so that you will have the right response for everyone.

- 1 JOHN 1:7 | If we are living in the light, as God is in the light, then we have fellowship with each other, and the blood of Jesus, his Son, cleanses us from all sin.

- PROVERBS 24:26 | An honest answer is like a kiss of friendship.

When you feel embarrassed by something your child has done . . .

- 1 JOHN 2:28 | Now, dear children, remain in fellowship with Christ so that when he returns, you will be full of courage and not shrink back from him in shame.

When you open yourself to others but they do not reciprocate . . .

- 1 PETER 3:8-9 | Finally, all of you should be of one mind. Sympathize with each other. Love each other as brothers and sisters. Be tenderhearted, and keep a humble attitude. Don't repay evil for evil. Don't retaliate with insults when people insult you. Instead, pay them back with a blessing. That is what God has called you to do, and he will grant you his blessing.

- COLOSSIANS 3:13 | Make allowance for each other's faults, and forgive anyone who offends you. Remember, the Lord forgave you, so you must forgive others.

As a parent of a child with special needs, do you ever feel you have special emotional needs as well? It can be so hard to share your family's story with someone new because it reminds you of the painful moments you've gone through. Perhaps you have been hurt by unkind or naive comments from others or even from well-meaning friends who give advice without fully understanding your situation. It can be difficult to open up and share life after experiences like these. The reverse can also be true, though. Perhaps you have a child who isn't able to reciprocate emotionally or verbally. It can be hard to give when you receive nothing back. Either way, God promises that these experiences can still have purpose. Bring your hurts to God so he can comfort you. When you're having trouble finding genuine community, hear God whisper to you, "Come and talk with me." In his fellowship you will find strength, comfort, and confidence to share your life with others and live in open, honest fellowship. You never know who will be encouraged by your story and example.

WAITING

When you're waiting for help to come . . .

- PSALM 40:1 | I waited patiently for the LORD to help me, and he turned to me and heard my cry.

- MICAH 7:7 | As for me, I look to the LORD for help. I wait confidently for God to save me, and my God will certainly hear me.

When you're waiting for results . . .

- PSALM 59:9-10 | You are my strength; I wait for you to rescue me, for you, O God, are my fortress. In his unfailing love, my God will stand with me.

When you're impatient with the timing of things . . .

- PSALM 37:7 | Be still in the presence of the LORD, and wait patiently for him to act.

- PSALM 57:2 | I cry out to God Most High, to God who will fulfill his purpose for me.

When it feels like God's help is too late . . .

- ROMANS 5:6 | When we were utterly helpless, Christ came at just the right time and died for us sinners.

- GALATIANS 4:4 | When the right time came, God sent his Son.

- 1 TIMOTHY 6:15 | At just the right time Christ will be revealed from heaven by the blessed and only almighty God, the King of all kings and Lord of all lords.

- EPHESIANS 1:10 | This is the plan: At the right time he will bring everything together under the authority of Christ—everything in heaven and on earth.

Problems always seem to arise at the worst of times, and it's in these troubled times that you learn that resolution is rarely instantaneous. Whether you're waiting for in-home care, a new therapy to begin, test results, or just to see progress, God knows what is happening, and the timing of his plan is always right. Keep crying out to God. Don't push to force results only God can accomplish. He gives you the strength to wait a little longer.

WEARY

When you're exhausted and need supernatural energy . . .

- PSALM 68:35 | God is awesome in his sanctuary. The God of Israel gives power and strength to his people.

- ISAIAH 40:29 | He gives power to the weak and strength to the powerless.

When your soul is restless . . .

- JEREMIAH 31:25 | I have given rest to the weary and joy to the sorrowing.

- MATTHEW 11:28 | Jesus said, "Come to me, all of you who are weary and carry heavy burdens, and I will give you rest."

When you wonder if your weariness is disappointing to others or God . . .

- PSALM 103:13-17 | The LORD is like a father to his children, tender and compassionate to those who fear him. For he knows how weak we are; he remembers we are only dust. Our days on earth are like grass; like wildflowers, we bloom and die. The wind blows, and we are gone—as though we had never been here. But the love of the LORD remains forever with those who fear him.

When you want to feel strong again . . .

- 2 CORINTHIANS 12:9 | Each time he said, "My grace is all you need. My power works best in weakness."

When you exhaust yourself trying to be the perfect example of a special needs parent . . .

- PROVERBS 23:4 | Don't wear yourself out. . . . Be wise enough to know when to quit.

- PSALM 91:1 | Those who live in the shelter of the Most High will find rest in the shadow of the Almighty.

When you're weary of facing the same struggles day in and day out . . .

- HEBREWS 12:3, 12-13 | Think of all the hostility he endured from sinful people; then you won't become weary and give up. . . . Take a new grip with your tired hands and strengthen your weak knees. Mark out a straight path for your feet so that those who are weak and lame will not fall but become strong.

Weariness happens for many reasons. Physical exhaustion, mental fatigue, health problems, stress from parenting, busyness, spiritual dryness—each of these can contribute to feeling weary. Many voices in our culture shout about how to heal the body and calm the mind, but only Jesus is your true source of strength and refreshment. When you call out to him, he reminds you he is right there with you and that his power is most evident when you are weakest. When you pray, he refreshes your heart with peace and renewed purpose. When you're disappointed, God lifts you up with tenderness and compassion. In times of weariness, go to God, tell him all your burdens, and share your heart. He promises rest, understanding, strength, and power to help you through each day.

WISDOM

When you want to make choices today that will still be good tomorrow . . .

- PROVERBS 1:23 | Come and listen to my counsel. I'll share my heart with you and make you wise.

- PROVERBS 16:1 | We can make our own plans, but the LORD gives the right answer.

- PROVERBS 9:10 | Fear of the LORD is the foundation of wisdom. Knowledge of the Holy One results in good judgment.

- JOHN 14:16-17 | I will ask the Father, and he will give you another Advocate, who will never leave you. He is the Holy Spirit, who leads into all truth. The world cannot receive him, because it isn't looking for him and doesn't recognize him. But you know him, because he lives with you now and later will be in you.

When you want your child to grow in wisdom . . .

- ECCLESIASTES 2:26 | God gives wisdom, knowledge, and joy to those who please him.

- PSALM 111:10 | Fear of the LORD is the foundation of true wisdom. All who obey his commandments will grow in wisdom.

- PROVERBS 15:33 | Fear of the LORD teaches wisdom; humility precedes honor.

- 2 TIMOTHY 3:14-15 | You must remain faithful to the things you have been taught. You know they are true, for you know you can trust those who taught you. You have been taught the holy Scriptures from childhood, and they have given you the wisdom to receive the salvation that comes by trusting in Christ Jesus.

When parenting a child with special needs goes beyond your wisdom and experience . . .

- PSALM 142:3 | When I am overwhelmed, you alone know the way I should turn.

- PSALM 18:30 | God's way is perfect. All the LORD's promises prove true. He is a shield for all who look to him for protection.

- JAMES 1:5 | If you need wisdom, ask our generous God, and he will give it to you. He will not rebuke you for asking.

- PROVERBS 3:5-6 | Trust in the LORD with all your heart; do not depend on your own understanding. Seek his will in all you do, and he will show you which path to take.

When you want your struggles to make you wise instead of bitter . . .

- LUKE 8:18 | Pay attention to how you hear. To those who listen to my teaching, more understanding will be given. But for those who are not listening, even what they think they understand will be taken away from them.

- PROVERBS 11:2 | Pride leads to disgrace, but with humility comes wisdom.

Navigating the world of special needs requires wisdom, doesn't it? What's the best way to talk to your child about his or her diagnosis? What's the best approach to therapy? What's the best way to encourage compassion among siblings and understanding among friends? How do you navigate awkward social encounters or difficult meetings at your child's school? These are all situations that require wisdom to know what to do. As you long for wisdom, first remember that Jesus is the source of all wisdom. He promises that those who follow him will be given the Holy Spirit, who provides us with the very counsel of God. Second, obedience to God's Word increases wisdom. Obeying him helps you know and recognize his voice when he speaks to your heart. He promises growth in wisdom to those who have humble and obedient hearts. Third, prayer increases wisdom. God doesn't resent that you don't always know what to do, and he loves it when you come to him for help! Your example in these areas is the best way to show your child the path to wisdom.

WITNESSING

When you need a story to tell . . .

- EPHESIANS 2:4-7 | God is so rich in mercy, and he loved us so much, that even though we were dead because of our sins, he gave us life when he raised Christ from the dead. (It is only by God's grace that you have been saved!) For he raised us from the dead along with Christ and seated us with him in the heavenly realms because we are united with Christ Jesus. So God can point to us in all future ages as examples of the incredible wealth of his grace and kindness toward us, as shown in all he has done for us who are united with Christ Jesus.

When you don't know what to talk about . . .

- PSALM 145:10-13 | All of your works will thank you, LORD, and your faithful followers will praise you. They will speak of the glory of your kingdom; they will give examples of your power. They will tell about your mighty deeds and about the majesty and glory of your reign. For your kingdom is an everlasting kingdom. You rule throughout all generations.

When you're afraid and you need divine initiative to share your story . . .

- ACTS 1:8 | You will receive power when the Holy Spirit comes upon you. And you will be my witnesses, telling people about me everywhere . . . to the ends of the earth.

- ROMANS 1:16 | I am not ashamed of this Good News about Christ. It is the power of God at work, saving everyone who believes.

When you wonder what causes others to believe . . .

- 1 CORINTHIANS 1:18 | The message of the cross is foolish to those who are headed for destruction! But we who are being saved know it is the very power of God.

When you want your life to reveal the love of Jesus to others . . .

- 2 THESSALONIANS 1:11-12 | We keep on praying for you, asking our God to enable you to live a life worthy of his call. May he give you the power to accomplish all the good things your faith prompts you to do. Then the name of our Lord Jesus will be honored because of the way you live, and you will be honored along with him. This is all made possible because of the grace of our God and Lord, Jesus Christ.

Witnessing can be scary. However, witnessing is simply living in a way that models Christ and sharing how you've seen God at work in your life. You and your child are a part of God's amazing story of hope, victory, and redemption. Some of your deepest struggles as a special needs parent may become the most powerful avenue through which God uses you to share his compassion and love with others. The power of your words and actions doesn't come from your effort, but from the power of God at work in the hearts and lives of those you come in contact with. Whether you share your life or your story, rest in God's power at work. His desire is for all to come to him.

WORD OF GOD

When you question if the Bible is relevant to your life as a special needs parent . . .

- ISAIAH 55:10-11 | The rain and snow come down from the heavens and stay on the ground to water the earth. They cause the grain to grow, producing seed for the farmer and bread for the hungry. It is the same with my word. I send it out, and it always produces fruit. It will accomplish all I want it to, and it will prosper everywhere I send it.

- HEBREWS 4:12 | The word of God is alive and powerful.

- 2 TIMOTHY 3:16-17 | All Scripture is inspired by God and is useful to teach us what is true and to make us realize what is wrong in our lives. It corrects us when we are wrong and teaches us to do what is right. God uses it to prepare and equip his people to do every good work.

When you wonder if you can trust in God's promises . . .

- ISAIAH 40:8 | The grass withers and the flowers fade, but the word of our God stands forever.

- ROMANS 15:4 | The Scriptures give us hope and encouragement as we wait patiently for God's promises to be fulfilled.

- PSALM 33:4 | The word of the LORD holds true, and we can trust everything he does.

When you want to hear God's voice . . .

- PSALM 119:24 | Your laws please me; they give me wise advice.

- JEREMIAH 15:16 | When I discovered your words, I devoured them. They are my joy and my heart's delight, for I bear your name, O LORD God of Heaven's Armies.

God's Word is forever. At the end of time it will remain as true as it is today. God's Word is alive and powerful, and God promises that wherever he sends his Word, it will be productive. Do you want to make decisions based on wisdom? God's Word offers counsel for wise living, helps you understand yourself, and will equip you for your role as a parent or caregiver. Most of all, it is God's voice proclaiming his heart. And the message of his heart is clear: You and your child are loved, you are worthy, and you are empowered! Let his Word be your joy and heart's delight!

WORDS

When you wonder if your words are getting through . . .

- PROVERBS 12:18-19 | Some people make cutting remarks, but the words of the wise bring healing. Truthful words stand the test of time, but lies are soon exposed.

- PROVERBS 10:20 | The words of the godly are like sterling silver; the heart of a fool is worthless.

- 1 JOHN 3:18-19 | Dear children, let's not merely say that we love each other; let us show the truth by our actions. Our actions will show that we belong to the truth, so we will be confident when we stand before God.

When you wish your child could understand what you're saying . . .

- 1 CORINTHIANS 13:1, 8 | If I could speak all the languages of earth and of angels, but didn't love others, I would only be a noisy gong or a clanging cymbal. . . . Prophecy and speaking in unknown languages and special knowledge will become useless. But love will last forever!

When others make insensitive comments about you or your child . . .

- 1 PETER 3:9 | Don't repay evil for evil. Don't retaliate with insults when people insult you. Instead, pay them back with a blessing. That is what God has called you to do, and he will grant you his blessing.

- PROVERBS 15:4 | Gentle words are a tree of life.

When you speak words of life . . .

- COLOSSIANS 1:6 | This same Good News that came to you is going out all over the world. It is bearing fruit everywhere by changing lives, just as it changed your lives from the day you first heard and understood the truth about God's wonderful grace.

Your words can either be noise in someone's ears or music to someone's heart. When you're frustrated with your child for ignoring you for the tenth time in a row, your gracious speech might be more powerful than a biting comment. When you're discouraged and feel hopeless that your child will ever have the speech skills to respond to you, you can speak love by gently caring and talking with him or her anyway. When others make cutting remarks, a gentle answer can transform their way of thinking. Your words reveal what is in your heart, so make sure your words reveal the wisdom, love, and graciousness of God.

WORRY

When you're worried about what will happen to your child . . .

- PHILIPPIANS 4:6-7 | Don't worry about anything; instead, pray about everything. . . . Then you will experience God's peace, which exceeds anything we can understand. His peace will guard your hearts and minds as you live in Christ Jesus.

- PSALM 55:22 | Give your burdens to the LORD, and he will take care of you. He will not permit the godly to slip and fall.

When you find yourself panicking over minor things . . .

- MATTHEW 6:25-27 | That is why I tell you not to worry about everyday life—whether you have enough food and drink, or enough clothes to wear. Isn't life more than food, and your body more than clothing? Look at the birds. They don't plant or harvest or store food in barns, for your heavenly Father feeds them. And aren't you far more valuable to him than they are? Can all your worries add a single moment to your life?

- PSALM 62:6 | He alone is my rock and my salvation, my fortress where I will not be shaken.

When there's so much that can go wrong . . .

- PSALM 91:2, 5-6 | This I declare about the LORD: He alone is my refuge, my place of safety; he is my God, and I trust him. . . . Do not be afraid of the terrors of the night, nor the arrow that flies in the day. Do not dread the disease that stalks in darkness, nor the disaster that strikes at midday.

When you're worried about what people think of you or your child . . .

- PSALM 149:4 | The LORD delights in his people; he crowns the humble with victory.

- PROVERBS 3:3-4 | Never let loyalty and kindness leave you! Tie them around your neck as a reminder. Write them deep within your heart. Then you will find favor with both God and people, and you will earn a good reputation.

When you want your thoughts to be at peace . . .

- PSALM 116:7-9 | Let my soul be at rest again, for the LORD has been good to me. He has saved me from death, my eyes from tears, my feet from stumbling. And so I walk in the LORD's presence as I live here on earth!

- 2 THESSALONIANS 3:16 | Now may the Lord of peace himself give you his peace at all times and in every situation. The Lord be with you all.

- PSALM 119:165 | Those who love your instructions have great peace and do not stumble.

At the heart of worry is the desire to understand and control the amount of difficulty you experience in life. Worry is a fear-driven emotion. But when things start to unravel, your fretting and panic cannot bring your much desired relief. When panic strikes, the key to a peaceful heart is remembering that you walk in the Lord's presence. He has been good to you and your child, and he remains your place of safety. He knows what you and your child need, and he is abundantly able and ready to provide. Trust in God as your strong foundation so you won't be shaken by the obstacles you encounter on the road of special needs parenting. May the Lord himself be your peace at all times and in every situation.